Bart King was two years old when he saw his first duckling. That little quacker was adorable! Between naps, Bart began learning as much as he could about cute stuff. Visit his **Cute!** blog at http://cute-overload.blogspot.com. (And don't forget www.bartking.net!)

OTHER TITLES BY BART KING
* ✶ Big Book of Girl Stuff
* ✶ Pocket Guide to Girl Stuff
* ✶ Bart's King-Sized Book of Fun
* ✶ Big Book of Boy Stuff
* ✶ Pocket Guide to Boy Stuff
* ✶ Big Book of Spy Stuff
* ✶ Pocket Guide to Brilliance
* ✶ Pocket Guide to Magic
* ✶ Pocket Guide to Mischief
* ✶ Pocket Guide to Games
* ✶ Big Book of Gross Stuff

All the best!

Cute!♥

A guide to all things adorable

Bart King

Illustrations
by
Jennifer Kalis

GIBBS SMITH
TO ENRICH AND INSPIRE HUMANKIND

Manufactured in Hong Kong in October 2011 by Paramount Printing

First Edition

15 14 13 12 11   5 4 3 2

Text © 2011 by Bart King

Illustrations © 2011 by Jennifer Kalis

Published by
Gibbs Smith
P.O. Box 667
Layton, Utah 84041
1.800.835.4993 orders
www.gibbs-smith.com

Designed by Rita Sowins / Sowins Design

Gibbs Smith books are printed on paper produced from sustainable PEFC-certified forest/controlled wood source. Learn more at www.pefc.org.

Library of Congress Cataloging-in-Publication Data

King, Bart, 1962–
  Cute! : a guide to all things adorable / Bart King ; illustrations by
Jennifer Kalis. — 1st ed.
      p. cm.
  Includes bibliographical references.
  ISBN 978-1-4236-2324-3
  1. Charm—Psychological aspects—Juvenile literature. 2.
Childishness—Psychological aspects—Juvenile literature. 3.
Aesthetics—Psychological aspects—Juvenile literature. I. Kalis, Jennifer.
II. Title.
  BH301.C4K56 2011
  111'.85—dc22

                                    2011009661

That's ME.

Hey!

**This book is
dedicated to
the cutest person
or animal
you know!**

Acknowledgements

Many thanks to the many delightful people who helped with this book, including Sarah Mead, Mary King, Celina Tobin, Tama Filipas, Bart King (not me, but the cool musician named Bart King), Laura O. Foster, Carol Guttzeit, Kevin Groh, Kristen Peterson McCormick, Alex Fus, Annemarie Plaizier, Robin Rose, Peter Andrews, Amy Baskin, Kelly Mucha, Bart King (yes, I just thanked myself), Megan Kelly, Angela O'Shea, Brandon Twine, Terry Brown, Kate Greenseth, Madeleine Levin, Tiffany Denman, Maya Holiman, Lynn King, Michelle Witte, Suzanne Taylor, and Madge Baird.

Contents

Things That Make You Say "Awww!"

✳ Cuteness is happiness ✳

Here's what happens when you look at an adorable baby or a cute koala.

* You get a warm, gentle feeling of affection.
* You start saying things like, "Awww!" or "What a widdle chubby-wubby!" in a high voice.
* You want to cuddle and look after it!

After all, these are the happy reactions that EVERYONE has when seeing something cute. That cute baby or animal sends us a powerful message: "I will make you love me."

Have you ever wondered how babies and koalas do this? And *why* are they cute in the first place? I mean, there must be reasons why one thing is cute ("puppy") but not another ("puppy poop").

To learn more about this, I borrowed Chudley, our neighbor's puppy, for a few hours. My goal was to carefully study Chudley to answer these very important questions.

But the only question I answered was, "Who's got the softest ears in the world?" (Answer: Chudley.) Since Chudley wasn't talking, I had to do some research. I learned that what you find cute can depend on two big factors:

1. *Your Friends and Family.* You usually agree with your friends on what's cute. Trust me, everyone does this. We agree without even noticing.

   Back when you were a baby, your parents and relatives talked about how cute you were. You eventually noticed this. Since your family had the good taste to think YOU were cute, you listened to their opinions about *other* things that were cute, too.

2. *Your Instincts.* Sometimes you naturally find something cute. It's part of who you are. After all, there are certain qualities that nearly *everyone* finds cute. And you'll find one on the next page!

   Ooh, here's an important thing to say: Cuteness isn't the same as Beauty. If something is Cute, we want to hold it in our lap and pet it. It might be clumsy and even sort of goofy-looking.

Cute Quality: Youth

Cute things don't HAVE to be young, but it helps! A scientist named Konrad Lorenz looked at cuteness. He saw that almost everyone automatically thinks babies are cute.

It doesn't stop there. Anything that even LOOKS like a baby is also cute. That's why so many baby animals are cute to us.

Baby humans don't *look* like babies for very long, though, and once they're adults, they're less cute. But there are animals that look almost the same no matter how old they are!

Panda bears are a good example of this. A baby panda looks a LOT like a little adult panda. The only difference is size. That's one reason why pandas are considered one of the cutest of all animals!

If something is Beautiful, we *admire* it. We might even be afraid of it. But Beauty is not clumsy and it's probably not even something we can hold on our lap.

Of course, if you hear a girl say, *"Mike is SOO cute!"* that's a totally   different meaning than what this book is about. (Unless Mike is a tiger cub.) But it IS true that most of what we consider "cute" is based on looks. Unfair!

How important are looks for cuteness? We know that babies are cute. But are some babies cuter than others? To find out, a bunch of babies were rated on their "cuteness" by a panel of judges.

It turned out that babies with high "cuteness ratings" got more eye contact and affection from their moms. That is *totally* unfair. It shows the danger of judging on looks. And it shows that if cuteness can affect the way a MOM acts, it's a very powerful force indeed!

So now we know that cuteness can make us happy. We also know that we have to make sure that cuteness doesn't make others UNhappy.

Anyway, cuteness isn't ALL about looks. Anything with a simple, goofy quality can be cute. For example, here is a cute joke that a girl told me:

Question: What did zero say to eight?

Answer: Nice belt.

✳ A Cute Word Is Born ✳

Words change over time, and "cute" is no exception. In the 1700s, cute was a spin-off from the word acute ("a sharp edge or point"). Back then, "cute" was defined as "clever or cunning, or sharp."

In the following years, "cute" went on to mean "smart-alecky." You know, like when an adult says, "Don't get cute!" to a little kid who's talking back.[1]

But for the last 150 years, cute has usually meant "pretty and charming in an innocent way." Of course, there are other words like this. For instance: *adorable, appealing, attractive, childish, comfy, comic, cuddly, delightful, engaging, free, friendly, frivolous, frolicking, gentle, genuine, happy, innocent, inoffensive, lovable, lovely, natural, precious, pure, silly, simple, sincere, soft, sweet, sympathetic, touching, vulnerable,* and *winning.*

Acute Dog   A Cute Dog

But cute is the handiest of them all!

✳ **Fun Fact:** The very first use of "cute" dates back to 1600. And it meant "a dog." (Of course, since dogs ARE cute, maybe this isn't that surprising.)

---

1. I like it when people tell me, "Don't get cute." ("You mean I'm getting cute? Finally!")

Cute Quality: Size

Small things are usually cuter than big things. Babies, pixies, puppies—they're all small. Why do we like small things? Maybe because they make us feel big!

Think of a little kid taking care of her doll. It makes her feel like a "big" girl. Cute things can't be TOO small, though. Not many people think germs or viruses are cute.

They're adorable!

So what is the smallest that something cute can be? If we say, "Anything as big as a Shetland pony to as small as a hamster is cute," that leaves out baby elephants and shrews. When a litter of baby shrews is born, they can all fit into a teaspoon. (Now THAT'S small!)

❖ **Fun Fact:** Some people find that *anything* tiny is cute: Little cans of soda, tiny cars, elephants that can fit in your hand, that sort of thing. But there is one small thing that is NEVER cute: fun-size candy bars. *Booo!*

Babies

Babies are irresistible. But why? Sure, they're young. But there must be more to it than that. Maybe it's the way a baby *acts*. Let's see, here's a checklist of baby activities:

☐ Cry   ☐ Barf   ☐ Poop pants

Sheesh! Luckily, babies also go to sleep. Then they wake up every two hours to cry, barf, and poop their pants some more. Plus, those little munchkins will stick ANYTHING into their mouths.

And if it won't fit, babies just drool on it instead![1]

With all this un-cute behavior, how do babies make our hearts melt? Maybe we HAVE to think babies are cute. Otherwise, we would avoid all babies, and humans would go extinct. **(Going extinct = NOT cute.)**

But fear of extinction isn't the ONLY reason babies are cute. It turns out that babies have a super-power: *They need our help*. And we find this hopelessly adorable.

---

1. Of course, babies grow up to be toddlers. That's when they start staggering around and smashing things.

Cute Quality: Helplessness

Whenever you see a helpless creature, your heart goes out to it. Not only do you want to help but you need to get your *heart back!*

So when Winnie the Pooh got a pot of honey stuck on his head, I felt sorry for him. Silly bear! I would have helped Winnie, too, but I didn't want to get sticky. Plus, he was in a book. (This posed certain problems.)

Human babies are so helpless, they can't even lift their heads in the beginning. As for being able to get that binky she dropped, forget it. Yes, babies need our help to survive, and we happily give it.

Useful Fact: When *you're* sick, your parents feel sorry for you. They can't help it. Look at you, so weak and helpless. This is why you should never *pretend* you're sick. (Unless it's important!)

Okay, so babies are cute just by being babies. We love to pick up the little tots and "coochie-coo" them. (Those chubby cheeks are irresistible.) Now here's a cute question: Have you ever seen a *toddler* come up to a baby to "coochie-coo" him?

A kid *you* once coochie-cooed is now coochie-coo-ing someone else. How cute is that? Crazy cute. I call this Multiplying Cuteness. Because when a cute kid notices that someone (or something) *else* is cute, the cuteness multiplies.

That's why little kids who play with babies or puppies or even just pick daisies make us feel *really* happy. It's true! When you look at babies, your brain *changes*. There is a chemical reaction in your head, and you actually FEEL different.

And it's a *good* feeling!

* **Random Cuteness** You're waiting in line to buy something. In front of you, a mom or dad is holding a baby who's peeking over their shoulder. The baby looks at you and smiles.

If we're *related* to the cute baby, we get an even stronger good feeling. To test this, a group of mothers smelled different pairs of stinky diapers. The mothers rated their *own* babies' diapers as less stinky than the others.

Were their own babies' diapers actually less stinky? Of course not! It's just that mothers thought their babies were so cute, their dookie didn't stink.

Of course, it's one thing to smell good, and another to BE good. We know babies are cute, but are they good? To test this, scientists carefully watched a group of one-year-olds while they watched a puppet show with *three* characters. One puppet was nice, one was neutral, and the last puppet was sort of mean.

After the show, all three puppets were placed in front of the babies. Almost all of the babies then picked up the nice character. They *liked* the "nice guy." The "bad guy" was almost NEVER chosen.

So maybe babies are naturally *good*. If so, that just makes the little munchkins even cuter.

YOU WERE A BIG BABY

A female gorilla usually weighs 220 pounds. A newborn baby gorilla (cute!) weighs 4 pounds. In comparison, human mothers usually weigh much less than 220 pounds. But their babies are usually *twice* as heavy as baby gorillas.

Ooh, I have to tell you what a man named Marcel Zentner did. First, he got 120 babies. Then Marcel started playing music for them. ALL kinds of different music, as long as it had a rhythm.

Then Marcel carefully watched the babies as they listened.

These babies couldn't waddle or walk or talk, but they COULD dance! Even though they were just little tykes, almost every baby would start to jerk around when the music was playing.

Were they great dancers? No. Were they CUTE dancers? Yes, they were!

Here's the best part: When the babies danced in rhythm and "nailed the beat," they smiled more! So babies naturally know how to dance . . . and they know when they are dancing well.

To put it simply: Babies rock. (And that's pretty darned cute.)

Cute Quality: Big Noggins

Big heads are cute!

Humans have really large brains. So a baby's head has to be HUGE to keep that big brain safe. What's interesting about a baby head is that it's sort of soft. See, our brains keep growing for the first months of our lives. And the plates of our skulls stay *flexible* to leave room for our growing brains.

So, compared to the rest of his or her body, a baby's noggin is colossal. Yet a newborn's face and jaw are baby-sized.

Since babies are adorable, we think: **Big Head = Cuteness!** Don't believe me? Look at the heads of your favorite cartoon characters. (I bet they're ginormous.)

Little Kids

So we know babies are cute. But toddlers, preschoolers, and grammar school kids are precious, too. In fact, I just saw a kindergarten class out on a field trip. The little boys and girls were all bundled up in puffy jackets and holding hands on the sidewalk.

One little girl was leading the pack. With her orange safety vest, she was bursting with pride at being in charge. As my eyes swept down the line of kids, it was fun to see how each one was cute in his or her own special way.

Finally, at the back of the line was a boy with an orange vest stretched tight over his huge down jacket. He had a worried expression as he waddled along like an overgrown duckling.

Why was HE so cute? I think I have it!

Cute Quality: Waddling

Any human or animal—or even robot—that waddles from side to side is cute. Why? Because it reminds us of the way toddlers walk. When a baby's learning to walk, she stumbles, toddles, tumbles, and rolls all over the place. Precious!

Toddlers are figuring out how to combine moves that we take for granted. It's actually HARD to walk. Next time you stand up and walk somewhere, think about every movement. You have to be balanced and coordinated to do it. And it takes LOTS of practice.

So when a toddler takes herky-jerky steps, there's a constant battle for balance. That's why a toddler doesn't move straight forward. Instead, he aims himself in one direction, but often actually walks in a *different* one. Cute!

That's why people find bears cuter than other big predators, like tigers. A bear can stand up on its back legs—like a person—and walk clumsily around—like a toddler.

♣ **Fun Fact:** E. T. waddled.

Isn't it amazing all the different ways that kids are cute? No? Sit down sometime and look at all the faces in ANY picture of an elementary school class. Even without knowing the kids, it's hard to keep a smile off your face.

Speaking of smiles, is anything cuter than chubby cheeks and dimples? I'll bet you find it hard to keep your hands off a chubby youngster or chunky puppy. Those folds of fat are redonkulous!

We like dimples because:

* Kids with chubby faces have them.
* They happen when people smile.

So we link dimples with children and good feelings.

Dimples are so cool, plastic surgeons sometimes get "dimpleplasty" requests. This is a surgery that adds dimples to a patient's cheeks. But with smiles AND frowns, those dimpleplasty dimples never go away. Permanent fake dimples? Not cute.

* **NOT cute!** *

* **Random Cuteness** Have you ever seen a little kid
STRETCHING to try and reach something on a high
shelf? (For some reason, this kills me!)

One thing that's really fun for a kid is acting like
a "big kid" or an adult. So when little kids talk on the
phone or get behind the wheel of the car, we elbow
each other and whisper, "Little Timmy is pretending
to drive the mini-van!"

This explains why kids put on tea parties. As a
child, I never understood WHY my sisters and their
friends would dress up and then pretend to drink tea.
It seemed pointless.

Yet now I see that it was fun for the girls to
imitate grown-ups. When kids do this, you almost
have to smile. But wait—none of the adults we knew

EVER threw tea parties. So WHO were the girls imitating? Oh well, embrace the mystery.

That reminds me of another part of cuteness: Playfulness. Kids can happily travel to an imaginary land where they must defend their magical fort from a slobbering monster. If the fort is made of sofa cushions and the slobbering monster is a Labrador retriever, that's not a problem!

* **Random Cuteness** Little kids jumping in puddles. Pure joy!

Speaking of games, try this: If you're playing with some children and it's time for a nap or bedtime, read them a story out loud. While you're reading, yawn a lot. The kids will start yawning too! Keep it up, and pretty soon you'll be treated to a cute sight: Sleeping children. (Note: This works great, but not on kids younger than five.)

Cute Quality: Contrast

A little kid is little.

I know, I know, that's obvious, but work with me here.

Since a little kid is little, she will look really cute if she holds or wears something BIG. So a five-year-old girl holding a giant inflatable killer whale is cute!

Anytime a little kid puts on something big, the contrast is funny AND cute. Like little boys in football uniforms: No matter how well the equipment fits, those helmets always look too big.

Even something as simple as a four-year old boy putting on his dad's shoes is cute. The bigger the shoes, the smaller the little kid looks—and the cuter he gets. When the toddler starts to toddle and shuffle and waddle in those oversized shoes, look out!

♣ **What About Captain Snow Mittens?** You may be wondering if there is a cute contrast when animals get dressed in human clothes. To find out, go to the Cuteness Courtroom (p. 35).

Animals

Animals are cute. And *baby* animals are SO cute, they have magic powers! See, I was just looking at a picture from Africa of a cute baby antelope. That little antelope was trapped by a group of cheetahs. Yikes!

Wait, stop crying—The cheetahs were *nuzzling* and *licking* the little baby antelope. Aww!

It turned out that the cheetahs caught the baby antelope just so they could admire its cuteness. Then the baby antelope started nuzzling the big cat's back. How sweet is that? Let's try to calculate it:

Cute animal + scary predator licking its face = Cuteness INFINITY[1]

I call this "the Lion and the Lamb" rule of cuteness. But what was it about the antelope that the cheetahs liked so much? Well, here's ONE thing!

1. Of course, it helped that the cheetahs weren't hungry.

Cute Quality: Fuzzy Furriness

* **Furball** *   * **Fuzzball** *   * **Snowball** *

Fuzzy-furry animals are cute. That's because they're fun to cuddle with. Even though most mammals have fur, they don't get to hog ALL the fuzz. Birds with downy feathers, like the Kiwi bird, are cute too. And baby penguins are REALLY cute.

Of all the eligible animals, which one has the most adorable, cuddly fur? Give up? It's the chinchilla! Once you touch this small South American animal's fur, you're going to need to dial 911 for a "cuddling emergency"!

♣ **Fun Fact:** Fruits vs. Vegetables — Not many vegetables are fuzzy, but Kiwi fruits and peaches prove there are cute fruits.

It's not just the way animals *look* that makes them cute. Their *behavior* is also important. For example, hedgehogs are REALLY cute. They're small and round and harmless and furry. But hedgehogs would

be even cuter if they would just SHARE the hedges and stop *hogging* them.[2]

So the way a human or animal acts can affect its cuteness. Toddlers are naturally precious. But if you ever saw one rubbing a crayon on your computer screen, you wouldn't think she was very cute.

A roly-poly, furry bear might be the same. We could assume that a fuzzy, round bear is naturally friendly, but this is unfair to the bear. It's a wild animal. The bear IS cute, but in its own, wild way.

I have to remind myself of this all the time. Since birds are cute, we have birdfeeders in our front yard. We watch goldfinches and hummingbirds hop and zip around. Then a troublemaker came and drove all the birds away. Bad squirrel! That bushy-tailed bandit was stealing all the seeds. He was NOT cute.

So I hung a birdfeeders way up high on the roof. Ha!

But the squirrel climbed up on the roof. Then it swung down from the rain gutter like a trapeze artist. Hanging upside-down by its toes, the squirrel kept eating seeds out of the bird feeder. Stupid squirrel!

This made me mad. But as I watched that stupid squirrel hanging by its toes, I found myself thinking, "Look at that! Heheh. Why that little rascal is actually . . . *cute?*"

I realized that I'd been thinking of the squirrel as my *enemy*. When an animal annoys us, it's harder to think that it's cute. That's just silly! The animal is still the same as before. It was my ATTITUDE about the animal that was the problem.

✳ Pets ✳

A pet is any animal whose job is mostly just to be cute. And since over 60 percent of U.S. households have pets, you probably know what I'm talking about. Of course, some people keep unlikely animals for pets, like crickets, crawfish, and tarantulas. (They're cute, too, if you're creative!)

Yet there's one animal that almost everyone agrees is VERY cute. That's right, I'm talking about *kitties*!

Cats have been kept as pets for the last 9,000 years. Wow! But I've only been studying them for the last 2,000. In that time, I've learned that a cat's fuzziness, personality, and playfulness make it irresistible. But wait, there's more:

1. The cutest and most precious cats are BABY cats. These are called "kittens." Kittens are incredibly rare.

2. Wait—never mind. It turns out that they're not that rare after all. But if you want to see something precious and rare, watch a kitten as it just wakes up from a nap OR is about to fall asleep. (*"So ti-wed!"*)

3. Kittens are adorable when they're playing with kitten toys or with another kitten. It is not QUITE as adorable if the kitten is playing with your nose when you're trying to take a nap.

4. When a kitten perches on something, that accents its cuteness. The perch can be something

like a little blue blanket (*"Widdle Kitty's on her blankie!"*) or a laptop keyboard (*"Widdle Kitty's on Facebook!"*).

5. 98 percent of kittens grow up to be cats. (Two percent become catfish!)

✳ LOLcats ✳

In 2006, a powerful new force of kitty cuteness entered the world: LOLcats (Laugh Out Loud cats). That's when the I CAN HAS CHEEZBURGER website started posting funny cat photos.

People would write captions of what the cat might be saying. But how does a human write like a cat? PUT THE CAPS LOCK ON. Also, pretend you don't know English very well. That means you should spell at least every other word wrong. (For example, use "Z" for "S".)

And be sure to use EXKLAMASHUN MARKZ!!!

Putting an "LOL" or "lol" in front of an animal's name has now become a password for online cuteness. There are now loldogs, lolbirds, lolhamsters, lolmice, and even the lolrus: "laugh out loud walrus"!

Walruses can be *really* cute. They're round and they look sort of cuddly. But walruses are so huge, they score sort of low in the "Harmlessness" category.

Cute Quality: Harmlessness

Which of these paired items is CUTER?

✳ A growling bear OR A playful bear?
✳ A playful bear OR A playful bear cub?
✳ A playful bear cub OR A snoring bear cub?
✳ A snoring bear cub OR A snoring bear cub wearing Star Wars p.j.s?

Did you usually pick the choice on the right? Me too! That's because the more *harmless* something is, the cuter it can be. This is one important reason why kittens are cuter than cats. *(Meowrrr!)*

And that's also why **sleepy** or **sleeping animals** almost ALWAYS get Cuteness Points.

As for **pajamas,** that's always a *major* bonus. Not only are they soft and comfy, it's hard to imagine anything scary that wears pj's.

❖ **Fun Fact:** Now you know why a puppy is so adorable when it rolls over and lets you rub its belly. What's more harmless than a rolled-over puppy?

Ooh, thinking of harmless animals reminds me of this poem from Japan:

Cuteness is the sound
Of ducklings on a pond
Splashing and quacking

Ah, ducklings. I think ducklings should be on the Cuteness All-Star Team. Why? Well, they are small, fuzzy, and rounded. Amazingly, the little quackers also have even MORE weapons in their cuteness backpack.

1. Ducklings waddle from side to side. Of course, ALL ducks waddle, but it's extra special with ducklings. Have you ever seen the little guys teeter-totter as they race along?

2. The little "quack" of a duckling might be the cutest sound of any animal, beating out a puppy's "arf," a kitten's "meow," and a baby's "goo"! (Also, just the word "duckling" makes me smile.)

3. Soon after it's born, a duckling will follow around almost anything that moves. This is usually the mother duck. What's cuter than a line of baby ducklings waddling in a row after their mom? I'll tell you: A line of baby ducklings waddling in a row after a black Lab.

"RUBBER DUCKY, I LOVE YOU"

In 1992, a ship in the Pacific Ocean suffered a tragedy. Almost 30,000 rubber duckies and other bath toys washed overboard. Because the duckies floated so well, many were found and scooped up, but it took 15 years for the last of the rubber duckies to wash ashore . . . in *England.*

I thought EVERYONE believed ducklings and other pets are the greatest. But women may find pets cuter than men. I mean, look at these numbers:

* 77 percent of veterinary students are women.
* 85 percent of the members of the Humane Society and the ASPCA[3] are women.
* 75 percent of litter boxes are cleaned by women.
* The odds that an adopted "rescue" dog is taken in by a woman are 11 to 1.

Of course, nobody's perfect:

* Women are twice as likely to dress pets up in outfits.

3. The American Society for the Prevention of Cruelty to Animals

You know, I've often wondered if this is okay. To find out, let's go to court.

The Cuteness Courtroom

The Question: Is it cute to dress up animals?

Judge Duckling: Will the defense go first?

Pug (rising): Your Honor, I argue that it IS cute to play dress-up with animals. As you can see, my owner dressed me in a pink tutu. How cute is that?

Cat: Objection! Look at the pug's face. Anyone can see how SAD he is to be wearing that silly dress.

Judge Duckling: Yes, he looks very sad. (Giggles) He's a sad little pug in a pink tutu! (Giggles harder)

Pug: It's true. I am a little sad to be wearing this tutu.

Cat: If letting your owner dress you up makes you sad, why do you let her do it?

Pug: To make her happy! When I look sad in this tutu, it just makes me even cuter. (Cat looks confused)

Judge Duckling: I am ready to make a ruling: If the pet doesn't MIND being dressed up, the results are CUTE. But if the pet resists the outfit, it is NOT cute and should not be attempted.

Cat (whispering to Pug): WHY would you try to make your owner happy?

Have you ever noticed how big a baby's eyes are? We are born with our eyes almost adult-sized. That makes baby eyes seem pretty enormous on the baby's face. Since babies are cute, that makes big eyes cute too.

A baby's big eyes are on the FRONT of its face and somewhat low on the head. Later in life, these same eyes will seem higher up on the face. But what *actually* happens is that a person's jaw and cheeks grow much larger as they get older.

* A "pupil" is the dark part of the eye. And eyes are a feature that makes critters cute. So which puppy is cutest? *

Pupil Size Is Important

Some animals—like terriers or prairie dogs—have eyes that are SO dark, they can look like "button eyes." That is, their eyes look a little like a stuffed animal's.

While I think button eyes are perfectly cute, other people don't. No worries! Everyone's welcome to their own cuteness opinion. (It's just too bad some people are afraid of stuffed animals!)

Besides clothes, why do we find an animal (like a panda bear) cuter than a fish (like an eel)? Yes, pandas are furry, but here are two MORE important reasons why a panda bear is so cute. Just look into its eyes.

* **The Eyes DON'T Always Have It** Just having big eyes isn't enough to be cute. I mean, giant squid have HUGE eyes. But while squids are very interesting, not many people find them very adorable.

How important are big eyes? It turns out that eye size is a huge factor when people give money to help animals. That means panda bears are great for raising money. Even though a panda's eyes aren't huge, it does have black fur patches around its eyes. These make the panda's eyes seem bigger than they are. People find that SUPER-cute.

* **Cuteness Bonus Round** An animal's cuteness can be doubled if it has its head *down* while it's looking *up* at you. Then you can practically hear angels singing.

I think that just the NAMES of some animal species are cute. For example, if you use the word "baby" or "pygmy" in an animal's name. Like with pygmy goats, pygmy pigs, or pygmy rabbits.

But back in prehistoric times, many animals had "wooly" or "cave" in their names, like wooly mammoths and Cave Care Bears. This made the animals sound more impressive.

"Make way, there's a wooly meerkat coming through."

"Watch your step, those are cave ducklings."

"Everyone run! A saber-toothed guinea pig is headed this way!"

These wooly cave animals were much bigger and fiercer than the ones we have today. So people back then had a different definition of "cute."

Can I keep him?

Of Mice and Men (Who Draw Mice)

"Keep it cute!" —*Sign that Walt Disney supposedly put over his artists' desks.*

Cuteness Experts (like us) study Mickey Mouse. It's not just that Mickey is cute. It's the way he *became* cute. You see, when Mickey Mouse started out in show business in the 1930s, he had a long, narrow snout, a small head, and small eyes.

Just like a REAL mouse!

With each new cartoon, Mickey's face changed. His head got bigger and rounder. His eyes got bigger. And his snout got shorter. In short, Mickey Mouse got cuter. As he got cuter, Mickey became more popular. (This was probably no coincidence.)

Bambi is another good example of a cute Disney character. When Disney artists first began on Bambi's movie, Walt Disney had them draw the baby deer as realistically as possible. But the artist's version of Bambi 1.0 was rejected.

That baby deer had to be CUTER.

So the artists shortened Bambi's snout, made his head bigger, and gave him eyes that were THREE times larger than a normal deer. Ta-dah! Now THAT was a deer that anyone could say, "Awww!" over.

Puppy Dogs

Is any animal as cute in as many different ways as the dog? I mean, big dogs (like mastiffs) can weigh over 200 pounds, but little ones (like Yorkies) might only weigh TWO pounds.

That means the size difference between an elephant and me is LESS than that between two dogs. Amazing!

There are fuzzy dogs, wiry dogs, and hairless dogs. Some dogs drool. Others don't bark. There are flat-faced dogs and dogs with long, narrow snouts.

Who's a good widdle puppy? You are! Is that ear itchy? Yes, it is!

BABY talk? In dog years I'm 42 years old!

There are fox-eared dogs, round-eared dogs, rabbit-eared dogs, and floppy-eared dogs.

Anyway, my point is that dogs have cuteness variety. People have enjoyed that variety for at least 14,000 years. (That's how long we've been keeping dogs as pets.) To prove how much we like dogs, think of all the baby talk they have to listen to.

Cute Quality: Ears

Because of the Power of Fur, animal ears can be cute in MANY ways. Small round ears (like an otter's) are cute, and long ears are totally awesome—right, Mr. Bunny?

Here are two cases of Ultra-Ear Cuteness:

1. When a dog (or other beastie) has ears that start out straight and then FLOP over halfway up, that's brilliant.

2. Dogs with just one floppy ear are cute-tacular.

Besides LOOKING cute, dog ears feel amazing. That's because the fur on a dog's ears is made from special velvet ear felt.

♣ **The Cutest Fabric?** Cuteness experts love fabrics like soft cotton, smooth satin, and velvety velvet, but they choose *felt* as the cutest of all fabrics. Not only is felt super-soft, it also gently sticks to itself . . . making it ter-rific for crafty projects.

How much do we like dogs? Well, people are three times more likely to give money to a person with a dog. And get this: women are about 20 percent more likely to go on a date with a man who owns a dog.

As you can imagine, people have their favorite dog breeds. To make certain breeds *sound* cuter than others, some cheaters put the word "toy" in a breed's name. Like the "English toy spaniel": Of course people will think it's cute.

As far as breed names go, I think the cutest one is the Otterhound. It's two cute animals at once. Also adorable is the Snorkie: a mix of a schnauzer and a Yorkie.

One dog that brings out the controversy in cuteness is the poodle. In the last sixty years, more than six million poodles found homes in the United States. This made them the most popular American breed by far. Joining them as super popular are cocker spaniels, Labrador retrievers, and beagles.

"Puddle of poodles"

Are poodles the cutest dogs because they're the most popular? Not exactly. It turns out that when it comes to picking pets, people often just copy what other people are doing. What's interesting is that they don't realize they're doing it.

Also, for every person who thinks poodles are cute, there is another who feels the opposite. This isn't the poodle's fault, though. The wild hairstyles that poodles are given at dog shows seem "disgustingly" cute to some people. But blame the owner, not the dog.

* **Skirting the Cuteness:** Poodle skirts are white or pink skirts with the silhouette of a French poodle on them. They may be cute, but some people think that Snorkie skirts are cuter.

MUTTS

Just as there are hundreds of breeds of dogs (purebreds), so there are mutts. These dogs are mixes of other breeds. Because you never know what a mix will look like, mutts can be cute in unexpected ways. You've probably seen Labradoodles before. They're poodle-Labrador retriever mixes. And I just saw a German shepherd-dachsund mix. It was as big as a shepherd, with really short legs. So it looked like a giant caterpillar.

Cute Quality: Noses and Mouths

Inside your nose is a firm tissue called "cartilage." When you were a baby, your nose
cartilage was soft. That's why babies
have soft little button noses. And of
course we think those noses are cute.
This affects how we look at animals
like the owl. It has a small nose— er,
beak. So most people find owls cuter
than big-beaked birds like eagles. (Of
course, animals with BIG noses —like baby
elephants— can still be cute.)

What kind of a story is that?

There is a legend about the dog's nose. In
ancient times, a dog was onboard a ship when
it spotted water pouring in through a hole. Thinking fast, the
dog stuck his nose in the hole.

The captain saw what happened, pulled the dog out of the
hole, and repaired the ship. Good dog! And ever since, dogs
have had cold, wet noses. (Look, it's just a legend, okay?)

Anyway, using "babies are cute" logic, small mouths
are also often considered cute. People who believed "the
smaller the mouth, the cuter" invented Hello Kitty (p. 110), a
cat with a mouth so small, it disappeared.

Of course, there's a reason why nobody ever created a
Hello Doggy. I mean, how would it bark?

ANTI-CUTE?

The last thing some people want is a cute dog. They want dogs that look TOUGH, like pit bulls, Rottweilers, and basset hounds. Of course, this strategy doesn't work that well. Even the toughest pit bull is cute when it's asleep . . . and hanging out the front of its muzzle is its cute pink tongue.

CHIHUAHUAS

These tiny dogs are SO small, they're almost cartoonish in their cuteness. Some people find Chihuahuas super cute, but other people strongly disagree. Does it help when Chihuahua owners carry the dogs in purses, dress them up, and constantly baby talk the dogs in public? To find out, let's go to court.

The Cuteness Courtroom

The Question: Are Furkids cute?

Judge Duckling *(looking at file)*: What is a "Furkid"?

Pug: Your Honor, a Furkid is a pet that gets treated like a baby.

(Judge looks puzzled)

Kitten: Have you seen little dogs being pushed in children's strollers? Or carried in purses? Those are Furkids.

Pug: And the Furkids lead happy lives inside their strollers.

Kitten: But if a dog is carried everywhere, when does it exercise? When does it meet other dogs? When does it smell dookie?

Pug: Maybe the Kitten is just jealous?

Kitten: What?

Pug: Cats NEVER get to be Furkids. They can't be trusted in a stroller. *(excited murmurs and catcalls)*

Judge Duckling: Order in the court! It's clear that Furkid "parents" love their pets and take good care of them. They may continue pushing their strollers.

(Pug high-fives an armadillo)

Kitten: But are Furkids CUTE?

Judge Duckling: No.

(Kitten high-fives the armadillo)

The Cutest Animals Hall of Fame

Four cuddly creatures are at the top of awards list for the animal kingdom. Here are my nominations:

4. Toughest of All Cute Animals: Penguin

I'll bet you didn't realize these comical birds were tough as nails, did you? They are, and I can prove it. Penguins can:

* hold their breath underwater for over 15 minutes.
* go without eating for *weeks*. (They live off their stored fat.)
* dive down to depths of well over 1,000 feet.
* live in gale force winds and freezing temperatures.
  Let's see a bunny do all of that.

As tough as they are, penguins are probably the best-loved birds in the world. Here are two cute things about them that you might not have known.

* Penguins waddle. (This is extra cute because penguins also have such excellent posture.)

But do you know WHY they waddle? Because it's awesome, yes, but also to save *energy*. Walking side to side burns fewer calories than a straight-ahead walk.

* Since penguins wear tuxedos, they sort of look like kids playing dress-up. It's believed that a penguin is black on the back so that when it's swimming, predators who are ABOVE it can't see the penguin because it blends in with the dark water. If a predator (like a leopard seal) is BELOW, the penguin's white belly helps it blend in with the sun and ice above.

3. Cutest Bear That's Not a Bear: Koala

Koalas AREN'T bears! Australians all know this, but it's common for non-Aussies to call these cute critters koala bears. (Just stick with the koala part.)

Koalas are marsupials, so they are more closely related to kangaroos than bears. Whatever they are, here are three reasons why koalas are SO cute:

* **Roundness** The body, head, ears, and eyes of a koala

are so round, the furry little guy almost looks like a cute cartoon come to life.

Baby koalas are called "joeys."

But I prefer "Joseph"

* **Sleepiness** A koala can sleep 22 hours a day. That means the koala might be the world's sleepiest animal. A sleepy koala is a CUTE koala.

* **Fur** If you think it would be fun to cuddle a koala, you're right. Although a koala can get a bit cranky when handled, its fur is apparently one of the lushest, most awesome furs of any marsupial.

2. Cutest Bear That IS a Bear: Giant Panda

While koalas aren't bears, giant pandas ARE. But they're not your average bears. For one thing, most bears—like grizzlies—eat meat. This makes a grizzly cute from a distance but scary close-up.

Giant pandas eat *bamboo*. Not scary! However, bamboo is hard to chew. (That rhymes!) To eat all the bamboo it needs, the giant panda has developed huge jaw muscles. These muscles makes the panda's head *big*. Cuteness score! It also makes the head look *round*. Double score!

I think the way that a giant panda eats is also cute. First, it likes to prop itself against a tree. Then it holds its bamboo with its front paws, which have "thumbs." So as the bear sits there shredding bamboo and eating, it looks sort of like a person.

As for its black-and-white coloring, giant pandas live in giant groves of bamboo. These groves have a lot of strong light and shade. So the panda's black-and-white fur helps it blend in with the surroundings.

On its face, the bear's black ears contrast with the white fur. Cute! And the black eye patches make the bear's eyes bigger. (I also think the patches make the bear look a little sad.)

✳ **Fun Fact** Other bears can do something cute that the panda can't: *hibernate.*

1. Cutest Marine Mammal: Which will it be?

"Dolphins. They think they're so cute. Oh, look at me, I'm a flippy little dolphin, let me flip for you." — Chum, *Finding Nemo*

There are LOTS of cute animals living in the sea.

I could write a whole book about porpoises, dolphins, whales, seals, and sea lions. Even killer whales can be cute. (The giant panda coloring pattern helps.)

But in my opinion, it's impossible to get any cuter than a baby harbor seal. First of all, ADULT harbor seals are really cute. They are sleek and round, and when the seals are on land, they are often sleeping.

When the harbor seals wake up, you'll notice they've got the cutest eyes of any animal. They're big and dark and wet. Oh, and their faces—harbor seals have cute whiskers and puffy cheeks. Their snouts somehow combine the cuteness of a cat and a dog. (Since harbor seals bark, maybe they are sort of like cute sea dogs.)

How do you make an animal this cute even *cuter*? Just imagine it as a BABY. Baby harbor seals have lighter fur with spots, sort of like the markings on a fawn. As for the baby harbor seal, don't look directly into its eyes . . .

The cuteness will burn you!

Cute Words

I love it when little kids talk in toddler-speak. You never know what they're going to say. Like when my four-year-old nephew explained to me about his hero's archenemy:

"And dat's why Batman has to look out for the Ribbler!"[1]

That was so cute, I laughed. I cried. I spilled my juice.

Besides mispronouncing, little kids like to use words that *sound* like the ones they're trying to say. Like saying "alligator" for elevator, or "copsicles" for motorcycle cops. Or the child who wanted more avocados for her salad and said, "More Colorados, please."

Then there's the little girl who watched *The Little Mermaid*. She asked about Ariel's outfit and was told that it was a "seashell bikini."

Baby talk is even simpler than toddler speak. Baby talk is the international language! That's because ALL babies babble the same way. It's not until they start

1. He meant the "Riddler."

learning words that they sound different.

The first sounds out of a little baby's mouths are vowel sounds (a, e, i, o, u). These are easy to make, like "*Aaaa!*" and "*Ooooo!*" The easiest consonants sounds include G, M, and D. So babies often say things like Googoo, Mama, and Dada. From there, a baby will start using baby-talk words, like "bun-bun" for bunny. (When a bun-bun eats a carrot, it goes, "*Nom-nom-nom!*")

Even as we get older, we still use baby talk with babies and animals. These words can even ease pain. I learned this after there was a tricycle accident in front of my house.

Little Kid: I skinned my knee—*Waaaah!*

Me: Did you get a booboo on your knee?

Little Kid (sniffing): Is it bleeding?

Me: Well, I can see an ow-ow right here. So I'm going

to throw it away. *(I make a fist over his knee, then lift my hand and make a throwing motion)* See? The bad booboo is all gone! Now it just needs wuv from your mommy.

Little Kid: Gee, thanks, lady. *(rides off on tricycle)*

Me: My name is Bart.

✳ **Learn a New Language** On really long car trips, kids learn to speak Whinese: *"Are we almost there?"*

Cute!

* Babykins
* Chunky Monkey
* Cuddle anything (ex. Cuddle Bunny)
* Lovebug
* Shmoopsie-poo
* Shnooky-pie
* Snookums
* Snuggle anything (ex. Snuggle Bear)
* Baboo
* Snuggles
* Squidge
* DillyDally
* Tweety
* Sunshine

Nicknames Gone Wrong

* Cutie Pants (avoid referring to someone's pants)
* Dearie (only okay for senior citizens)
* Tootsie (see "Dearie")
* Buttercup (see "Dearie" again)
* Twinkles (ugh)
* Doll-face (used by old-time gangsters)
* Ladybug (do you want someone to "fly away home"?)
* Lamby-pie (vegetarians and sheep dislike this)
* Love-chunks (ALL chunks are BAD chunks)
* Poopsy Woopsy (ALL poopsy is BAD poopsy)
* Sugar Booger (no explanation needed)

✳ Cute Nicknames ✳

Our dog is named Ruby, but her nickname is
Cinnamon Bear. (Tell me that isn't cute.) That's
because words like "bear," "angel," or "baby" often
work well as nicknames.

* **Cutesification** You can often "cutesify" a word just
  by adding an "-ie", "-y," or "-ette" to its end!

  But be careful when picking a cute nickname.

Getting Cavities

* Gumdrop
* Honey Bunny
* Sugar anything
  (Sugar Bear, Sugar
  Dumpling, etc.)
* Sweet anything
  (Sweet Cheeks,
  Sweetie Pie, Sweet-
  ums, etc.)

Mischievously Cute

* Bumpkin
* Pookenstein
* Dumpling
* Goober
* Troll
* Munchkin

Baked Goods

* Crumpet
* Muffin
* Cupcake
* Shortcake
* Pudding
* Dumpling
* Honey Bun
* Nutmeg
* Snickerdoodle

Produce

* Apricot
* Peaches
* Pumpkin
* Cabbage

"Angel face" or "baby boy" are fine, but "angel breath" or "baby brain" seem a little odd. To help you choose, use the chart on the previous page that people call their babies and pets . . . and sometimes even each other!

Besides being adorable, cute names can be important. That's why companies choose their names carefully. Sounding cute can really help business. I mean, think of Apple, Twitter, Google, and Yahoo.

✳ **Barbie the Barbarian?** The name Barbie comes from Barbara. The name Barbara means "outsider." And it comes from the same Greek word (*barbaros*) as "barbarian."

I've always wondered why nobody has named a company Baby® yet. I mean, everybody already likes babies and anything baby-related. The Germans have a good word for this: *Kinderschema*. It means that we will automatically like anything that reminds us of human babies.

✳ Cute Words ✳

There are all sorts of words that are cute. Like "smushables." These are the snacks that you pack on top of your lunch bag so that they don't get *smushed*. And, of course, we can combine words into phrases.

Sprog: to go faster than a jog but slower than a sprint.

Wibble: The trembling of the lower lip just shy of actually crying.

WARNING: The following phrases are pretty cute.

1. **"Are you snug as a bug in a rug?"** This is a good thing to say to kids as they go to sleep. If they say, "Yes," ask them what kind of bug they are.

2. **"Chunk-tacular chub-roll"** Useful for describing the fat rolls on a baby or a puppy.

3. **"Pretty Little Pony"** Toy ponies can have a powerful effect on young girls. I was reminded of this when reading a news story about a "suspicious" toy pony that was found near an elementary school in southern California. The suspicious thing about the pony was that it was just sitting there. So police officers placed explosives next to the toy pony and then blew it up. Noooo! (The pony was later declared "non-threatening.")

＊ **Random Cuteness** Here are some cute band names:
Chumbawumba, Tummy Ache, Raggedy Ann,
Huggie Bear, Crayon, Cute Is What We Aim For, Goo
Goo Dolls, Bananarama, and the Go-Gos.

Do you know what "terms of endearment" are?
These are words like "darling" and "baby" that people
use for their little cuties. For example, Germans
might call their dear one *liebe*, but in Spanish you
could say *bomboncito*: little marshmallow.

For some reason, French is a good language for
this sort of thing. For added cuteness, just add the
word petit ("little") in front of any noun. So *"Ma
poupée"* (my doll) becomes *"Ma petite poupée."*

Practice with these:

Mon bébé: My baby

Mon canard: My duck

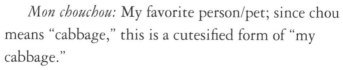

Mon chaton: My kitten

Mon chéri: My dear

Mon chouchou: My favorite person/pet; since chou
means "cabbage," this is a cutesified form of "my
cabbage."

Ma crotte: My "dropping." This can also mean a
small, round goat cheese.

And in case you're wondering, the French word
for "cute" is *mignon* (mean-yon). Hey, here's another

cute foreign word: *Kumbayah*. Haven't you ever sat around a campfire singing, "Kumbayah, my Lord, kumbayah"?

I have. In fact, I'm doing it right now. Oh, no—my marshmallow burned again.

Is *kumbayah* an exotic word from a distant land? Not really. Kumbayah comes from the lingo of folks who lived off the coast of South Carolina. For them, "kumbayah" meant "come by here" (as in *"Come by yah"*).

Hey, now the song sort of makes sense. Anyone got some more marshmallows?

I guess if a word I didn't even understand can be cute, then almost anything can be cute.

—Wooly caterpillars? Cute!

—A log that looks like a monkey? Okay!

—Hey, there goes a balloon! So cute!

Punctuation marks can even be cute.[2] Look, here are two people high-fiving: o/\o

And that brings me to the cutest punctuation sign of them all!

2 Except these: #*?

Cute Things

SMILEY FACES

The odds are that if you see someone—or something—smiling, you'll have good feelings. This is why people like hippos. You see, hippos have huge mouths, and if you look at them, they always seem to be smiling. Of course, hippos are also round, pudgy, and they have big heads, so that doesn't hurt.

The famous smiley face was invented by an artist named Harvey Ball in the early 1960s. Ball got $45 to come up with a yellow button that had two eyes and a smile. *Ho-hum.* ☹

Then in 1970, three guys dug up his classic smiley face and added the slogan *"Have a nice day."* Score! ☺

Within two years, the smiley face ended up on about 50 million different buttons, bumper stickers, key chains, etc.

Soon, that smiley face would become the most massively popular emoticon EVER. ☺

✳ Cute Handwriting ✳

Just the way words LOOK can be cute. I've even known some people (usually girls) who practice their

"cute handwriting." You laugh, but cute handwriting can make things happen. Japan is the world capital of cuteness (see p. 106). And the Japanese cuteness craze got started around 1970 with a cute style of handwriting called things like *burikko-ji* ("fake child writing") or *koneko-ji* ("kitten writing").

Kitten writing. I like that.

Teenaged girls started the fad by writing all their notes and letters in the round, little-kid characters of *koneko-ji*. The girls also drew little stars, hearts, and cartoon faces in with it. By 1985, over half of all teenage Japanese girls were using "fake child writing."

Can you guess what happened next? Some girls began *talking* and *dressing* like little kids, too. So clothing companies started making little-kid clothes in BIG-kid sizes. Today, the Japanese teenagers who write, dress, and talk like little kids are doing something called *burriko suru*, "acting like a fake child."

Cute Sounds

Being around cuteness can change the way that we act and think—and TALK. Have you ever noticed that when someone is talking to a cute baby or an adorable kitten, they speak three octaves higher than normal?

That was a big burp for such a little pumpkin!

* **Cute Tip** Want to talk in a cute voice? I have ONE word for you: Helium!

As for kids, they have naturally high voices. That makes almost anything they say cute. But my favorite is when a child imitates an animal.

Cute Quality: Laughter

Is there anyone who DOESN'T love hearing peals of happy laughter? I didn't think so. Of all the chortles and guffaws out there, the sound of a baby chuckling is the cutest.

Mwahahaha!

And when we hear a baby laugh, we laugh as well.

Well, we USUALLY laugh.

People are naturally drawn to humor and laughter. We all like to smile. And when we laugh, it's pleasant and rewarding. It just feels good.

Laughter is SO awesome, I even like seeing "LOL" in messages. BTW, did you know that kids in France use MDR instead of LOL? That stands for *mort de rire*, or "dead from laughing."

Hmm. You know, let's stick with LOL.

❖ **LOLs Across the World** In Thailand, the number five is pronounced "ha." So 555 is used for LOL!

You: What sound does the cow make?

Darling Child: "Moooooo!"

You: Right! And how does the monkey go?

Darling Child: "Eee-eee-eee!"

You: Good. And what does the duck say?

Darling Child (pauses): "To the best of my knowledge, a duck cannot speak."

Ha! Hey, this reminds me to always "play along" with kids. They don't have to be correct ALL the time.

You: Look, a train! What sound does Mr. Train make?

Toddler: Chugga, chugga. Wooh! Wooh!

You: Please. Modern trains have diesel engines. They sound nothing like that.

✳ Furry Friends ✳

When a cute animal makes a cute sound, you get a double-whammy of cuteness. And like so many things, the babies often make the cutest sounds. For instance, adult meerkats sound *mere-ly* adorable. (Oh, snap!)

But baby meerkats (or meerkittens) are in a dimension of cuteness all their own: *Adorabubbleness*.

Meerkittens squeak out pitiful little squeals that tug the heartstrings of anyone who hears them. Because of this, the meerkittens get spoiled rotten by the whole meerkat colony. Everybody swings by to give the crying babies food for the first three months of their lives.

What's funny is that the meerkittens will continue squeaking even after they're old enough to go get the food themselves. So right around the 100-day mark, the adult meerkats stop giving in to the young ones. Why? The little kittens' voices have deepened. So even though they're still awfully cute, the meerkat youngsters have to feed themselves.

After checking in with a panel of experts, I've narrowed down the Cute Sounds Award Winner to four finalists:

4. Have you ever heard a duckling quack? Then you know why it's here!

3. When it comes to sheer cute awesomeness, it's tough to count out a cat that's **purring** contentedly.

2. There's only ONE furry little animal that can **whistle, purr, chatter, AND burble**: the *guinea pig.*

1. But the Cute Sounds Award Winner is a quietly snoring dog. It can be very soothing to hear a dog snore, and almost any  sleeping animal is cute. But snoring dogs can also be entertaining to watch when they run after bunnies in their dreams.

I DISAGREE

"If dogs could talk, it would take all the fun out of owning one." —Bob Dylan

Pink: Cute or Not?

I think that almost any color CAN be cute. That's why rainbows are so awesome. They have all the colors of the . . . rainbow.

Choose any color in the rainbow. Now picture that color in its most delicate, shimmery version. What you're imagining is the PASTEL version of that color. Pastels can be really cute. For instance, a soft yellow pastel seems cozy and cuddly. An orange pastel might be fun and playful. And a light red pastel can be . . .

Pink is for Romance

Aaargh!

PINK. The natural enemy of boys!

Why do boys have pink-ophobia? It must be because pink is a girls' color.

Except it isn't!

True, pink is not thought of as a MANLY color. Soldiers don't have pink guns. Construction workers don't wear pink hard hats. And if a boy in first grade wears a pink shirt to school, you can bet one of his friends will say, "Pink is for girls!"

✳ **Pink Dolphins? The Chinese white dolphin can be pink, and a bubblegum-pink bottlenose dolphin lives north of the Gulf of Mexico.**

It does seem like almost every little girl goes through a "pink phase." (This often happens when the girl takes her first ballet class.) But it hasn't always been this way! Back in the 1800s, it was common for both girls and boys to wear little white dresses! And the girls and boys *kept* wearing the white dresses until they were about five years old.

By 1900, improvements in dyes made it easier to make clothes with colors. So leaders in the clothing and greeting card businesses got together and decided *pink is for boys and blue is for girls.*

Did you see that? Parents started dressing their boys in PINK! That's because pink was considered the "baby" version of red, which was a strong, manly color. Girls were encouraged to wear "baby" blue, because it was dainty and delicate. If you look at classic Disney films, you can see what I mean. Blue outfits for girls are featured in *Cinderella* (1950), *Alice in Wonderland* (1951), *Peter Pan* (1953) and *Sleeping Beauty* (1959).

But by 1960, the color assignments slowly began to reverse to pink for girls and baby blue for boys.[1] And that's why pink is thought of as a "girly" color today. This is, of course, very silly. So the next time someone says baby girls naturally LOVE pink, you can say, "A girl *might* naturally love pink . . . but she might also like any other color too."

As for the guys, any man who wears pink is showing he's a confident person. He takes risks and doesn't take himself too seriously. Boys who wear pink are brave enough to not care about peer pressure—or *jeer* pressure.

✳ Think Pink ✳

Not everyone likes pink. Take, for example, the baby pink flamingo named Little. He was born at the London Zoo. To get Little to eat, the zookeepers used

1. One reason for the switch was art. Henry Huntington (1850–1927) was a very rich man who bought two portraits of a girl and a boy. The paintings were called Pinkie (of a girl dressed in pink) and Blue Boy. The two famous paintings hung next to each other in a museum.

What's Your Favorite Color?

Why do you like certain colors and dislike others? Sometimes, it's because of your life. If you adore your older sister and her room is all green, then the odds are that you'll like green as well. But if you were once bitten by a green cat, you might not like green at all.

Fun Color Facts:

* Blue is a popular color everywhere in the world. (Being the color of the sky and water has advantages.)
* Dark yellow and brown are not super-popular colors anywhere. (Pee and poop may explain this.)
* People who like school almost always like their school colors. (Surprise.) They might also dislike the colors of their school's rival.

a hand puppet that looked like a grown flamingo, but Little was terrified of it.

After trying some different things, the zookeepers realized it wasn't the sock that Little was afraid of—it was the color PINK. You see, when pink flamingos are born, they are covered with a whitish-gray down. It takes up to a year for their pink feathers to grow in. So as Little grew older, he got used to seeing more and more pink, and he got over his fear.

After the Boston Red Sox won the 2004 World Series, pink Red Sox hats became popular. So people with pink hats were thought of as fans that had "jumped on the bandwagon." Some believed they were not "real fans" that had suffered through all of the previous 86 seasons without a championship. (As one person said, *"Nobody suffers in pink."*)

So in Boston, the phrase "pink hat" came to mean anyone who was a new fan in ANY sport.

Pink can also stand for MANY other things, like:

* Equal rights.
* Support for women with breast cancer.
* The Hot Pink Grannies. This is a basketball league for senior citizens. The players wear hot pink skirts and tights.
* Calm. Football coach Hayden Fry had the locker room for the visiting team painted soft pink. That's because it's a relaxing color, which wouldn't help the visitors play good football.

Shiny Stuff

As a writer, one of my greatest strengths is being able to focus and not get distracted—
Look, something shiny!

Pause

I'm back. The shiny something turned out to be a DIME. *Yes!* That's ten cents for me. Hey, you know what else is shiny? Glitter.

Glitter has ALWAYS caught people's eyes. Ancient cave people might not have thought bunnies were cute, but they DID like glitter. We know this because bits of a shiny mineral called "mica" have

Look at that glita. So pretty!

been found in prehistoric cave paintings. Putting mica in the paint gave the pictures a cool, sparkly quality.

But who wants to grind up rocks to get glitter? Not me!

Now this glitter timeline will give us some more sparkling highlights.

30,000 years ago: Edible glitter is made from food coloring and the sap of the acacia tree. While this glitter isn't tasty, it IS biodegradable.

1934: It only took 30,000 years to figure out that glitter can also be made by grinding up brightly painted plastic. That's where most of our glitter comes from today. Because the pieces of glitter are so small, most people don't realize that when glitter is not cleaned up, it can be accidentally eaten or become pollution. That's bad for everyone.

1960s: Cosmetics makers add glitter to lipsticks and eye shadow. Few people want to put plastic on their faces, so cosmetics makers start using sparkly fish scales instead. (Really.) But instead of calling it "fish scales" they call it "pearl essence" or "pearlescence."

1990s: A major GLITTER CRAZE takes off in middle schools. Glitter pens and sparkly wands are the big items, and some girls even put glitter in their hair and on their faces.

2006: Glittery versions of My Little Pony are introduced. The sparkly little colts are so cute, even cave people would be impressed.

But while glitter is glittery, sometimes you need a BIGGER glitter! That's where the shiny discs called **sequins** come in. You've seen sequins in clothes, accessories, and jewelry. Dancers and other performers love them because sequins (a.k.a. spangles) reflect more light than glitter.

∗ In The *Wizard of Oz* movie, Dorothy's ruby slippers are covered with sequins.

Back in the old days, kings and queens wore sequins made from flattened gold. And gypsies wore gold coin sequins on their belts and blouses, which is pretty cool. But if you see a sequin today, it's probably just made of plastic.

So I guess all that glitters is NOT gold—and sequins are just giant chunks of glitter!

Surprisingly Cute

Do you know what makes me smile?

Yes, my mouth. (Very funny!)

But something else that makes me smile is things that *aren't* cute . . . but actually ARE. For example, Heidi, the cross-eyed possum!

I like possums, but SOME people think they look like giant rats that only come out at night. So how could a cross-eyed possum be lovable? Heidi is a cross-eyed possum for whom the *opposite* is true.

Possums get around in the dark, and they also rely on their sense of smell. So having crossed eyes isn't a problem for Heidi. When a German zoo began taking care of her, videos of Heidi became super popular. People flipped out over that adorable, cock-eyed marsupial. I mean, Heidi even got her own plush toy. She was a cuteness star!

So what WAS it about Heidi that made her appealing? Read the next page to find out.

All this just goes to show that cuteness isn't always logical. In fact, it's probably fun to have a cute-ugly dog as a pet. People (like me) stare at it in shock, and then want to learn more about it. This broadens our definition of what cuteness is.

For years, I've wondered why **troll dolls** are cute, but now I'm starting to get it. You've seen troll dolls before, right? They're those pot-bellied little dolls with messy, brightly colored hair. Why are trolls cute? Well, they smile a lot, which is always nice. Being small, round, and harmless doesn't hurt. And although the original troll dolls were carved out of wood (back in 1959), today's trolls are made of soft, rubbery vinyl.

But of course, trolls are also U-G-L-Y. As we're learning, that might be what makes the trolls cutest of all.

Now let's dip our toes into the water for our next surprisingly cute creature: jellyfish. By now, you

Cute Quality: So Ugly It's Cute

A monster attacked me the other day. Luckily, it was a *small* monster.

This beast looked like a child's night-mare. It had a black, barrel-like body, the ears of a rabbit, and the face of a hobgoblin. Grunting like a pig, the horrible creature ran up to me and bounced off of my leg.

As it came back again, I could see its barrel bottom shaking frantically back and forth. Hey, the little monster was wagging its behind!

"Sorry," said a man, running up and putting a leash on it. "Lily just likes to say hi." Sensing my amazement, he added, "Lily's a French bulldog."

I looked down at the hobgoblin. Its head was split by an enormous mouth and its little eyes were shut with glee. It was a DOG? But Lily was hideous!

And really, really, REALLY cute. Lily was the best! She taught me that some animals can be SO incredibly ugly, they are beautiful. You know, like bats, baboons, and that kid down the street.

Hideous creatures remind us that being different isn't just okay—it's *awesome*. (Just ask Lily!)

❖ **Fun Fact** June 26th is National Ugly Dog Day (aka, National *Cute* Dog Day).

know many of the elements of cuteness, but jellyfish don't really match up with ANY of them. I mean, jellyfish have no visible eyes, they are not fuzzy, and some even have tentacles with deadly poison. Yeesh.

Even so, some people find jellyfish cute. Maybe it's because jellyfish are soft and round and slow, and even sort of graceful. I suppose that having the word "jelly" in a name doesn't hurt.

It seems like a lot of the animals that live in water are surprisingly cute. Like the **octopus!** Of course, an octopus does have a big head and big eyes, which are two parts of cuteness. But suckers? Tentacles? And beaks are fine on parrots, but on an octopus?

Even so, there's just something really great about an octopus, and "cute" is the only word I can think of to describe it.

Another sea creature I should mention is the **sea-horse**. It IS cute, but why? I mean, isn't a seahorse just a big head with a tentacle tail? Yet there's something small and dainty and amazing about seahorses. Maybe it's the S-shape. And since they're sort of a small, water version of a horse, seahorses seem a bit magical. One person explained it this way: *"I think it's that seahorses are miniature horse mermaids."* That's perfect!

This is a good chapter to mention how **pigs** break ALL the cuteness rules. They have small eyes, big snouts, and roll in the *mud*. A pig's head is big, but it just sort of merges with its neck. The grunts and squeals a pig makes aren't adorable. Finally, pigs are stubborn, independent, and NOT very helpless.

Why are pigs so cute? They just are. Pigs are funny and they have pink snouts. Plus, *oink*s rule! Hey, that reminds me of a cute pig joke: How do you keep a pig from oinking in the back seat of your car? Let it sit in the front!

Oink! Oink! Oink!

Cute Quality: An Interesting Wrinkle

At first, I didn't think that loose, wrinkly skin was very cute, but have you ever noticed how babies are so pudgy, their skin is folded, wrinkled, and puckered? It turns out that lots of animals have loose skin when they're born.

Babies and young animals NEED loose skin so that they can grow properly. That way, when the baby or puppy has a growth spurt, it has something to grow *into*. Then there are animals—like Shar Peis—that keep loose skins throughout their lives.

Oh, and there's on more wrinkle to the cuteness of loose skin: When you look at a chubby baby that looks like the Michelin man, the loose skin makes the tyke look even rounder. Round is cute, too!

❖ **Fun Fact:** Older folks have loose-fitting skin. So does E.T.

For some reason, pigs remind me of another strangely cute animal: the **manatee**. While cute things are often small, manatees are BIG. They're three times bigger (and 20 times heavier) than an adult human. Size aside, the manatee is a slow-moving, gentle giant that loves to have its belly scratched.

Manatees are so lovable, I'm shocked when someone finds them ugly. Part of this has to do with familiarity. People who aren't USED to seeing manatees might think that they're disturbing. And so many people only seem to find "famous" animals cute. It turns out that even wildlife experts prefer to study more glamorous animals (like leopards) instead of cute-ugly ones like warthogs and manatees.

Strangely Cute—Mushrooms

Why mushrooms *shouldn't* be cute:
* Mushrooms are fungus. *Fungus?*
* Not only that, they grow from spores. *Spores?*
* Mushrooms can sometimes even be poisonous. *What?*

Why mushrooms are *cute anyway*:
* They're soft and round.
* Mushrooms seem to appear out of nowhere, like magic.
* Pixies like to use mushrooms for furniture.
* The Mushroom Kingdom is a fun place for Mario to bound through, as he jumps on all the Goombas and Koopa Troopas!

Anyway, there are MANY animals that I'm feeling alone in finding cute. Ooh, like **pelicans**. They're big and their heads are long and narrow, but pelicans are also clumsy and even goofy-looking. Maybe that's why I like them so much.

Here's one more animal that *shouldn't* be cute but is: **A kid getting into mischief!** For instance, say your four-year-old brother decided to brightly color his entire body using orange and blue ink markers.

He's almost done when you walk in. Your brother looks at you and freezes. YOU freeze too, because at first, all you can see is an orange-and-blue munchkin.

Then you laugh.

Why? Just look at that colorful gnome. You just can't help it. He may be in trouble, but he's just so stinking *cute*. This is the same reaction we have when kids decide to make Mom and Dad breakfast in bed. Everyone knows it's going to be a messy disaster, but the little chefs are so innocent, it's adorable anyway.

✳ My Favorite Unexpectedly Cute Animal ✳

I love all animals, cute or otherwise, but my very favorite cute animal lives in a group of lakes in central Mexico. It's a salamander known as the Mexican axolotl

(ACK-suh-LAH-tuhl). Some people don't believe sala-manders are cute because they think they're slimy. This is not true; the axolotl lives underwater, so it's WET.

Here's why this Mexican salamander is cute:

* The axolotl has magical-looking feathery gills that surround its head.
* It can be black, white, and even pink.
* Like pandas, the axolotl looks the same as a baby as when it's an adult.

The only thing NOT cute about axolotls is that human pollution has made them an endangered spe-cies. Like so many animals, the axolotl needs our help to survive. And if we can give that help, it's not just cute. It's AWESOME.

Cute Things That May Not be Cute

Lots of things can be cute, but some stuff is just too BIG to be cute. You know, like outer space. Or the ocean. Or weather.

Wait. I guess *parts* of the weather can be cute. Like fluffy white clouds. And rainbows. Ooh—and snow. Snow is fluffy and white . . .

＊Surprising Fact: Weather CAN be cute!

Okay, I didn't think things like the stars or the sun could be cute. But now that I think about it, cute "sun" artwork has been attached to refrigerators with magnets for a long time. How did all these magnet artists make the sun cute? What is their secret?

＊ Making Things Cute ＊

To find answers, I interviewed an artist named Chloe. She is five years old. We recently sat down over glasses of apple juice.

Me: Chloe, Your pictures are very good.

Chloe: Thank you.

Me: So, in this picture, you've drawn a hill, the sun, and a pineapple. All of them are cute. What is your secret?

Chloe: Faces.

Me: Huh?

Chloe: I draw faces on stuff like candy, cars, and clouds.

Me: Of course! Do the faces always smile?

Chloe (shakes head): Watch. *(draws sun picture above)*

Me: A person's face looks sort of weird on something that's not a person.

Chloe (nods): Now look. *(draws sun picture below)*

Chloe: See how the sun beams?

Me: So when drawing a cute face on an object, a simple face is better. Chloe, you're a genius.

Chloe: Thanks. Want more apple juice?

Chloe taught me a lot. For one thing, I need to ease up on the apple juice. She also told me that a picture's **caption** can change its feeling.

Imagine a picture of a puppy on his back, next to a sofa. Different captions send different messages.

Helpless: "Me fall down!"

Clever: "Who hit the 'paws' button?"

Ironic: "You dare to laugh? Your destruction is assured."

Of course, puppies are always cute no matter WHAT the caption. But there is one animal that doesn't fall in the same category:

✳ The Unicorn ✳

Unicorns aren't cute. I know, I know. That seems wrong. We're used to seeing lovely white unicorns running through flowery meadows with rainbows arcing behind them. In fact, that's what I see when I look in my backyard each morning. (I live by an imaginary wildlife preserve.)

But baby unicorns ARE cute.

While a unicorn is majestic, regal, and awesome, it's NOT cute.

Unicorns are big, strong, and fast. And they're not even harmless! How many cute animals have a big sharp horn coming out of their heads?

For years, people thought of unicorns as white horses with a twisted, light-colored horn. Unicorns were believed to be magnificent wild animals that could only be tamed by innocent young women.

But why would you WANT to tame a unicorn? It'd be nice to have one as a pet, I guess. (I'm not sure how well a unicorn would get along with my hamster, though.) Anyway, the first description of a unicorn dates back more than 2,300 years. The ancient unicorn was believed to be from India. It had a short, dark horn, the body of a horse, the tail of a boar, and the head of a deer.

And the unicorn bellowed![1]

As you can see, an animal can be beautiful and awesome, but not cute. I think that noble creatures like rhinos, tigers, and even whales are like this. And that reminds me of an interesting rule about cuteness AND beauty. We like to see things that look the same on both the left AND right sides.

1. Cute things don't usually bellow. (Hey, do you know what a baby unicorn is called? A uni-colt!)

Cute Quality: Balance

Cute Unbalanced   Uh-oh!   Hey, who let the bunny in?

When it comes to cuteness, we look for balance or symmetry. That means we want our puppies to have an ear on one side of its head. And, like a mirror image, there should be an ear on the other side.

Sometimes, if we upset the balance a little, it can be unexpectedly cute. But when things get REALLY unbalanced, look out!

That's why people almost always rate "balanced" faces as cuter than less-balanced ones. We link balance with health. So we notice right away if someone or something has blotchy skin or patchy hair. We usually think of cuteness as something that healthy young people and animals have.

When we see something that's balanced, it seems simple and easy to understand. Just like cuteness!

❖ **A Mystery Revealed** Boys usually HATE it when their relatives call them "cute." They don't want to be thought of that way. But here's what's funny: After the boys become men, they don't mind it anymore!

Here's an odd question: Have you ever been afraid of a doll?

I have!

My sister had a doll that was *really* scary. First, this doll was BIG. It was almost the size of a real kid. Second, it was very realistic. And third, this doll was made out of wood. This was totally unlike the soft, stuffed dolls—like the GI Joes—that I normally play with.

Then my sister set this spooky doll up on a high shelf in her room. So if you went in her there, a giant, real-looking girl was looming above you, looking like she might leap down as soon as you turned your back.

This made me nervous when I had to go into my sister's room to wake her up or read from her diary.

I mean, dolls are SUPPOSED to be cute! But as we know, cuteness has certain qualities. So if a doll fails to be cute because it's too big, or its eyes are too close together, or WHATEVER, our brains get confused.

That's when a doll goes from cute to *spooky*.

One great thing about dolls is that they are terrific sidekicks. I mean, if you've ever seen a girl pulling a wagon with a doll riding in it, you can tell who's in charge. The doll is her sidekick! And sidekicks can be cute because they are usually smaller and/or younger than us. That means we get to be the boss. (Just like Batman!)

One of the cutest kinds of sidekick is a pet that looks like its owner.

Sometimes a sidekick can even be a younger kid who looks and dresses like you. But do you think a doll that looks and dresses like you would be cute? Just imagine opening a package with a Mini-You inside. You pull yourself out of the box and look at you. Freaky!

There is a company that makes dolls like this. You pay for the doll and then send in a photograph of yourself. When your Mini-Me arrives, you activate your doll by talking to it. As you do so, the doll's voice-recognition software enables it to speak in YOUR voice!

Yikes— I just got goosebumps imagining my Mini-Me talking to me in *my* voice. That's the second time that a doll has gone from cute to *spooky*!

If a talking doll isn't necessarily cute, what about a talking animal? I've seen videos of dogs who can sort of say, "I ruv you!" and that's adorable. But when it comes to talking animals, I think parrots. So I visited my friend Kurt. He has a big gray-and-red parrot named Zane.

"Parrots are very cute," Kurt said. "They're clever, unique, and brightly colored. And Zane says funny things all the time."

"Good to know," I said, taking notes. "Hey, Zane, will you talk to me?"

Zane cocked his head at me. What a pretty bird! "Help! They've turned me into a parrot!" he answered.

Wow! I looked over at Kurt, but he just laughed. So now I'm not sure if that was the cutest OR most disturbing thing I've ever heard an animal say.

This all has me thinking about the nature of cuteness. Oh, and it looks like it's time to go back to court.

The Cuteness Courtroom

The Question: Are horses cute?

Kitten *(rising)*: Your Honor, it was shown earlier in this very chapter that unicorns are not cute. And what is a horse but a unicorn without a horn?

Pug *(rising)*: Objections! First, that rhymes. Second, it's ridiculous. Your Honor, girls have loved horses for ages.

Kitten: But since when do GIRLS decide what's cute?

Judge Duckling *(long pause)*: Er . . . since ALWAYS?

Pug: Your Honor, think of a horse's muzzle. It's velvety soft. And a horse has HUGE eyes.

Kitten: Fine. But don't horses sometimes buck off their riders? Hmm? *(murmurs are heard in the courtroom)*

Pug: I'd like to enter this photo into the evidence. *(Pug hands photo to Judge)*

Judge Duckling: Oh, my. Look at that!

Kitten *(craning neck)*: What is it?

Pug *(taking back photo)*: Oh, it's just—*(dramatically holds up photo)*—a picture of a little PONY. *(Chaos breaks out in the courtroom as everyone starts pointing and shouting, "Look at the pony!")*

Judge Duckling: Clear the court!

Un-Cute Quality: Twee

When someone tries too hard to MAKE something cute, it just ends up as cutesy instead! (In other words, *anti*-cute.) There's even a word for this sort of cutesy anti-cute: *twee*!

Going From Cute to Twee

Naturally Cute

Twee!

The word "twee" came from toddlers *trying* to say the word "sweet." Today, twee is used to describe anything that's sickly sweet. And when it comes to serving twee, baby photographers take the cake. As we know, babies are born cute. So if a photographer tries too hard to make a baby even *cuter*, the result can be the reverse of what was intended.

Polka Dots

Of all patterns, I think polka dots are the most jolly. That's why almost nobody is ever in a bad mood when wearing polka dots. (And if they ARE, they look very silly.)

Polka dots are simple, friendly, and fun. Maybe it's because the dots are happily bouncing around. Cute!

But polka dots used to be VERY un-cute. If a person got a disease like measles or smallpox, their skin broke out in spots. In the days before good medical care, even just ONE dot was thought of as scary. That was because one dot suggested there might be MORE dots soon.

Since dots were often linked to disease, nobody would have dreamed of making fabric with dots on it. That's why no Europeans wore dots in the Middle Ages. A very few did put on *stripes*: Criminals and clowns!

Dots weren't considered bad everywhere. For African bushmen, dots showed the amount of a person's magic. The more dots, the better.

You know a "dot" on a girl's face is called a beauty mark. The idea that a face dot IS beautiful comes from about 400 years ago in France. That's when a tradition called "patching" began.

The idea with patching was for a girl to stick one little dot of black fabric on her face. If she had perfect skin, that little dot would call attention to her beauty. Later, these face patches got really popular. Girls even started using star and crescent moon shapes as well as the dots.

Speaking of popular, Europeans started going wild for polka music in the mid-1800s. Polka music is cheerful, and polka *dancing* involves a lot of smiling and little jumps. Somehow, the cute dance became linked with the cute dots, and next thing you know—polka dots were born.

Of course, the new polka dots were just dots, but

what a cool new name! "Polka dots" have been super-popular with kids and adults ever since. They ended up on sheets and clothes for kids *and* adults.

✳ **Fun Fact** In 1962, a comic-book hero named Polka Dot Man was introduced. His secret weapon: Magic polka dots. (Don't ask!)

Cuteness Super-powers

We already know that cuteness can give us all a warm, cheerful attitude. Cute things also make it easier for us to socialize. After all, loving cute things is something all of us have in common. That makes a puppy the perfect icebreaker.

But is that all cuteness can do? No. *Being* cute gives an adorable animal—like a guinea pig—cuteness superpowers. And *looking* at that cute guinea pig gives you incredible abilities, too. Don't believe it? Read on.

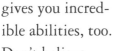

✳ Superpower I ✳
Making the World a Better Place

Because cute things are innocent, we have kind feelings for them. That means:

MORE CUTENESS = MORE KINDNESS

Yay!

✳ Superpower II ✳
Defense

Guinea pigs, babies, and bunnies all share a special superpower: defenselessness. Because they can't defend themselves, we want to keep them safe.

Man: Help! Angry wolverines are threatening my baby bunny.

You: A bunny? *(courage surges through you)* Maybe I can help.

Man: Agh! Now a hungry bear is growling at little Bun-Bun.

You (racing in and saving the bunny): Here's your bun-bun, sir.

(Grizzly and wolverines snarl in disappointment)

You: And here's a carrot for YOU, little feller.

Bunny: *Nom, nom, nom*

So, it turns out that being defenseless is actually a very good defense.

Cute Usefulness?

Do you know anyone who pretends not to understand cuteness? Maybe it's a person who thinks cute animals are useless. "Sure, a guinea pig is cute. But what is it *good* for?" [1] Down in Peru, there's a town called Pachacama that runs on guinea pig power. Yes, when the people living nearby watch TV or turn on the lights, guinea pigs make that happen. Not this way:

The guinea pigs are kept on a ranch, where they're fed especially good food. Then someone collects the guinea pig poop and uses it to create energy. How much poop can 1,000 guinea pigs make? Oh, about three tons!

1. Like it's an animal's job to make itself useful to humans!

✴ Superpower III ✴
Making People Better

Have you heard of the kids' game called "Operation"? If you've never played before, here's how it goes: You have a pair of tweezers. Using these, you pretend you're a doctor who is picking up small objects. But if your hand shakes, you set off a buzzer. So steady hands and concentration are the keys to playing well.

Anyway, a bunch of people once played "Operation." Afterward, they were sorted into two smaller groups. One group of players was then shown cute pictures of cats and dogs. The other group was shown REALLY cute pictures of kittens and puppies.

Then everyone went back and played Operation

again. Guess what? The people who looked at cute pictures of cats and dogs did better. They had good focus and their hands were steady.

And the people who looked at kittens and puppies did a LOT better.

So cuteness makes you more alert and helps you concentrate. (Seriously.) That means when people wake up in the morning, they should look at *cute things*. No more coffee and doughnuts![2]

This Cuteness Superpower can help us care better for babies. After all, babies are delicate. To take care of them, we need to be careful.

When you look at a baby, you are under the influence of its cuteness. That cuteness makes you a better babysitter. This helps you do things like fastening the baby's buttons (cute!), holding its bottle (adorable!), and wiping its little bottom (well, two out of three isn't bad).

Some people have reported feeling weak in the knees when holding a baby bunny. Does cuteness actually make you weaker? No. But it DOES make you less likely to exert your full strength so you act more tenderly with the baby bunny.

2. On second thought, let's keep the doughnuts!

✳ Superpower IV ✳
Reducing Stress & Unhappiness

Since dogs are cute, being around them is good fun. One person describes just *looking* at pictures of puppies as "Relaxing. It's pure happiness." So what happens when you get to actually PLAY with a dog? It's awesome, and this is especially true when we are stressed out.

High school and college students get REALLY stressed out during final exams. After all that studying, they just need to clear their minds for a moment. That's why some schools bring in dogs during finals week. Then the students can set down their laptops to pet and play with some puppies.

This really is good science. Your body has lots of different chemicals in it. Some of these chemicals can make you feel stressed. Others can make you feel good. When you pet a dog, your body's stress chemicals go *down*. At the same time, your "good mood" chemicals go *up*. Amazing!

Want to learn something even more amazing? The exact same thing happens to the dog. So dogs really DO like to be petted. How cool. What other animal calms us down and cheers us up at the same time?

Of course, "therapy" dogs also go to hospitals and rest homes to make people feel better. This seems fun for the dogs, too. You may have noticed that lots of dogs are happiest when they have a job to do.

And sometimes that job is just licking a sad person's face.

✳ The Ups and Downs of Cuteness ✳

Despite all that good news, being cute isn't all sunshine and flowers.[3] Just ask any baby! Some days, that bottle just doesn't taste good. If being cute is so great, why don't YOU try wearing dirty diapers for a while?

UPS!

* People smile at you automatically.
* Being cute is awesome.
* You are pleasantly plump.
* You're always a hit at a party.
* You're adorable.

DOWNS!

* You're never taken seriously.
* People pinch your cheeks.
* If ONE more person calls you the Michelin Man, you'll poop your pants.
* Will the baby talk EVER stop?
* Where will you keep all the hearts you've stolen?

3. Actually, being cute pretty much IS all sunshine and flowers, but I'm trying to make a point here!

Cute Super-Quality: Curiosity

Dogs are curious about the world. Especially when they're puppies. When a bunch of puppies scamper around, they're trying to see, smell, and chew everything they can.

This makes us laugh, but it does more than that. Watching a puppy, we imagine seeing the world through its eyes. The puppy's exploring gives us a fresh new look at our surroundings.

Now look at a baby or toddler the first time she goes to a petting zoo or sees a waterfall. When you see the look of wonder on a child's face, it's cute. It's touching. And it reminds us of the **wonder** we should feel every day for the world around us.

If THAT'S not a superpower, I don't know what is!

There is one other downside to being cute. When a politician runs for election, he or she LOVES to be shown holding babies. The idea is that *anyone* who likes babies has to be okay. (Yes, I know this is silly.)

But if the politician has a BABY FACE, that is not helpful. That's because voters usually prefer to vote for candidates who look "adult." Baby faces need not apply!

Japan

✳ The Cute Capital of the World ✳

Cuteness is loved all over the world, but is it loved with the same affection everywhere? Not really! Think of cuteness like candy. No matter where you go on the planet, you will always find some candy there. But in some countries, people eat MORE candy than in others. They have a bigger candy appetite. The same thing is true of *cuteness*. And no nation has a bigger appetite for it than Japan. It's the cute capital of the world.

The Japanese cuteness craze started about 1970

and has been going strong ever since. (I call Japan "the Land of the Rising Cute.") To label all the cuteness they were creating, the Japanese began using a special word for it: *kawaii.* It is one of the most used and loved words in Japan.[1]

Over time, Japan's kawaii spilled over its borders. In nearby nations like Korea, Thailand, Indonesia, and Taiwan, kawaii is VERY popular. And Japan's biggest kawaii stars are known everywhere. I mean, you've heard of Sonic the Hedgehog, the Mario Brothers, the Pokémon monsters, and Hello Kitty, right? Hey, it looks like a list is creeping up on us!

✳ Six Ways That Japanese Cuteness Is Unique ✳

1. TEENAGERS (AND SOME ADULTS) TAKE IT SERIOUSLY

People of all ages love cute stuff, but little kids are usually the ones who are most affected by it. For instance, you might have had Winnie the Pooh pajamas or a SpongeBob SquarePants lunch box when you were 6, but would you still use them when you're 16? Probably not!

1. Kawaii comes from the Japanese word kawayushi, meaning "shy" or "embarrassed."

Here's why: teens often want to be treated like *adults*. So many teenagers rebel against "rules" and try NOT to act like little kids. That means ignoring the precious, fun, and cute stuff of childhood.

In contrast, a Japanese teen might happily carry a lunch box while wearing pajamas. That's because being treated as an adult may not be all that great. There is a belief in Japan that for a teen to "grow up" means hiding behind an artificial layer of adulthood. Which means the precious, fun, and cute stuff of childhood is lost forever—*unless* teens hang onto it. So they sometimes do.

* **Fancy** **Cuteness has a big impact on teen fashion in Japan. These fashions can include puffy sleeves, ruffles, frilly lace, and LOTS of ribbons.**

Some adults worry this shows that Japanese teens don't want to grow up at all. Others think it's just a unique part of their culture. Which view is correct? I'm too busy picking out a good lunch box right now to decide.

2. MASCOTS

In Japan, EVERYTHING gets a cute mascot. For example, Japan is broken up into 47 areas called "prefectures." (These are like states or provinces.)

Each prefecture has its own cute mascot. Of course, pretty much everything else has its own mascot, too. Companies, road signs, and even police stations all have a cute little creature that symbolizes them.

The idea is that these mascots give an organization more personality and can even make them seem less threatening. Ads for the Japanese military even show cuddly cartoon characters.

Together, these symbolic mascots are called *yuru-kyara.* And every year, there are competitions that decide who are the cutest among them.

Just like Japanese cartoon, comic-book, and video game characters, the yuru-kyara often have these features:

* Colored hair (often green!)
* Tails
* Antennae or rabbit/cat ears
* School uniforms
* Mammoth eyes or tiny, button eyes
* Giant hands and feet
* Fur

3. HELLO KITTY

Japan is full of dreamy mascots with their heads way up in the fluffy, fluffy clouds. Maybe the most famous of them is a white cat with a bow on her head—and no mouth!

Wait, where did Hello Kitty's mouth go? One spokesperson for the mascot said she HAS a mouth but it's "hidden in the fur." But another Hello Kitty creator said the cute cat doesn't have a mouth because she "speaks from the heart."

You know, that's a pretty good excuse.

The Hello Kitty story goes back to 1960. That was the year a man named Shintaro Tsuji started a company called Sanrio. At first, Sanrio sold greeting cards, but soon it specialized in something called "character merchandise."

In other words: *cute mascots!* There have

been LOTS of Sanrio mascots, like Vanilla Bean, Duckydoo, Button Nose, Tiny Poem, and the Little Twin Stars. But the queen of them all is Hello Kitty!

After her "birthday" in the mid-1970s, Hello Kitty became incredibly popular just for being herself. Her main job over the years has been to appear on products. In fact, Hello Kitty has been on over 20,000 different ones. They include:

* fly swatters
* candy
* credit cards
* surfboards
* vacuums
* body-fat monitors
* guitars
* spatulas
* cell phones

* motor oil
* purses
* cars
* toilet paper
* bibs
* clothes
* lunch boxes
* $30,000 diamond watches

Maybe it'd be easier to mention products Hello Kitty WON'T appear on: strong alcohol and weapons. (And I have yet to see Hello Kitty litter!)

The white cat from Japan is so popular, there are even Hello Kitty cafés. In Hong Kong, a TV newscaster named Wincy Miaow even hosts The Hello Kitty Weather Report. But it's hard to top the Hello Kitty hospital in Taiwan.

✳ **Define "person"** Hello Kitty is so popular in Taiwan, she was voted the island's third most popular "person" one year.

As patients enter the Hello Kitty hospital, they see a statue of the cat in a doctor's uniform. From there, every surface is pink and/ or Hello Kittified. She's even on the hospital's birth certificates! The hospital director said, "I wish that everyone who comes here . . . can get medical care while seeing these kitties and bring a smile to their faces."

Sayonara!

Goodbye Kitty

✳ **Twins?** Hello Kitty has a twin named Mimi. How can you tell the two apart? Mimi always wears her hair ribbon on the RIGHT side of her head, silly!

4. MANGA

Manga books are the hugely popular graphic novels from Japan. They are designed to be read in reverse—from the *back* of the book to the front—and the pages are read from *right* to *left*, not left to right. Why? Because that's how the Japanese read.

If you've seen the manga style before, you know that the characters are usually drawn with HUGE eyes. That's why manga books are sometimes called "big eyes save the world." This art style came about during the late 1800s, when Japanese leaders encouraged the Japanese people to imitate Western culture. You name it, they copied it.

There are different types of manga. One that is often called "cute" is *shojo* (or *shojo shumi* or even *shoujou*). Since *shojo* means "girl" in Japanese, you can guess whom these are intended for! *Shojo* stories are usually romantic and innocent, and most of the readers of *shojo* are tween and teen girls. The publishers of most manga books label them with age suggestions.

5. MUSHI

Japanese kids love lots of "creepy-crawly" critters. That's because the Japanese have a tradition called *mushi*. It has to do with the world of insects. But not just ANY insects! The idea is that BIG bugs like stag beetles, cicadas, grasshoppers, ant lions, crickets, and fireflies are the most interesting. So Japanese kids collect, trade, and keep them as pets. *Mushi* can also include tadpoles, lizards, and salamanders. Taken together, all these animals are thought of as totally cute.

The kids who are into mushi are often boys. One of their favorite activities is giving a piece of watermelon to two giant beetles to see whose bug can shove the other away and eat the melon. Although a rhinoceros beetle is fearsome looking, it's quite

harmless. And even though it's big for a bug, a stag beetle is actually pretty small.

There are LOTS of stores that sell mushi animals, mushi cages, and mushi food. There's no doubt about it: *mushi* are cool—and cute. They can also be expensive: Some purebred beetles have cost thousands of dollars.

6. VIDEO GAMES

If you've ever played video games, you know about one of the first and most popular ones ever: Pac-Man. After it came out in 1980, players fell in love with the Pac-Man character. It was a little strange, since Pac-Man was just a round yellow circle that ate dots.

Pac-Man was made by a Japanese company. Soon, other Japanese video games followed, like Donkey Kong, the Legend of Zelda series, and of course, the Super Mario Bros. Obviously, not ALL video games were cute, but a lot of the first ones were. And not ALL video games come from Japan, either, but a lot of the cutest ones have. (To this day, the newest video games usually come out in Japan first.)

From the very beginning, Japanese video games used the cuteness qualities you've learned about. As more and more games were created, there's never a shortage of characters with big heads and giant eyes.

* **A Long Tradition of Play** When Nintendo went into business in 1889, its first products were playing cards.

Part of the reason for the look of video game characters was practical. The early games were *very* low-resolution. There weren't many pixels to work with—so Mario got a big head (to exaggerate his collisions), a big mustache (because his mouth couldn't move), and a cute red hat (because his hair couldn't move!).

Of course, video games are designed to make money. To make MORE money, video game characters are constantly jumping into cartoons, movies, comic books, and other merchandise. Like toys!

* **Lemon meringue pie** *

* **Pac-Man pie** *

Toys

I think the cutest toys are stuffed animals. It's so adorable when a Japanese baseball player hits a home run and someone hands the slugger a plush stuffed animal as he crosses home plate. And have you ever noticed in ice skating championships that people in the crowd give their favorite skaters a plush animal?

Oh, and notice the word "plush." Have you ever noticed that ALL stuffed animals are fuzzy?

The King of the Stuffed Animals must be the Teddy Bear. These toy bears owe their name to U.S.

president Teddy Roosevelt. In 1902, a newspaper comic came out showing Roosevelt refusing to shoot a cute baby bear. (This was partly based on a true story.)

So a New York store put a toy bear in its display window with a sign: "Teddy's Bear." The rest was history! A teddy bear craze swept the United States, and it seemed like every child had to have one. As a result, teddy bears came to symbolize innocence, childhood—and *cuteness!*

＊ **Interesting** From an early age, girls show much more interest in stuffed animals than boys.

If your teddy bear was stressed out by that, just send it on vacation. There is a travel company that does "Teddy Tours." All you have to do is mail your teddy bear to its destination. Once it gets there, your teddy bear gets to stay in a hotel and get photographed doing fun things. For instance, if you sent your teddy to Finland, the bear would come home with photographs of it hanging out with reindeer and going on snowmobile safaris. I don't know if this is cute or crazy—or both.

Whenever I think of teddy bears, I always think of Ewoks. If you've seen *Star Wars: Revenge of the Jedi,* you know that Ewoks are basically walking teddy bears. I mean, look at those big button eyes! And

that's not all,
they have these
features as well:

Size: small
Shape: chubby
Ears: small and
round—like a bear!
Limbs: short
Appearance: furry
Hobbies: hang gliding
(just like teddy bears!)

✳ **Fun Fact** Ewok children are called Woklings.

✳ Some Cute Toy Crazes ✳

Part of the fun of stuffed animals, dolls, and action
figures is that you get to boss them around. Along
these lines, a group of dolls named the **Cabbage
Patch Kids** came out in 1982. These dolls came with
their own adoption papers. Owners of the dolls could
be serious about pretending to be parents.

The "adoption paper" strategy worked like a
charm—the Cabbage Patch Kids were a huge hit and
became hot collectors' items. Of course, other toys
have started their own "cute crazes" over the years.
Here are a few of them.

1996: The plush doll Tickle Me Elmo had a cute secret weapon: If you rubbed his red tummy, he would laugh and laugh and laugh. This Sesame Street character was so popular, he created Elmo-Mania. At one store, there was even a stampede for the "must-have" doll. When Tickle Me Elmo sold out, it was a cute tragedy.

1997: The Beanie Babies were nine different little animals stuffed with plastic "beans." They were soft, colorful, and small. A trick used was "retiring" older Beanie Babies while releasing new ones. This encouraged collecting. The Beanie Babies were pioneers for later Internet-related toys like Webkinz and Neopets. Some Beanie Babies had creative names, like Chocolate the Moose and Radar the Bat. But Pouch the Kangaroo? Nuts the Squirrel? Someone's not trying hard enough.

1999: The Furby was a little robot that looked sort of like a hamster with a beak. When the toy was first turned on by its owner, the Furby spoke a cute gibberish called Furbish. (No, I am not making this up.) As the Furby's owner talked to it, the little furball learned new words and phrases. This made the Furby the first robot toy to become a HUGE hit.

1999: Kids already knew about the Pokémon (cute little monsters that had morphed from animals and plants) from Nintendo's video games, but in 1999, *Pokémon* cards and stuffed animals were suddenly EVERYWHERE. This was the first time that a video game created a hit toy.

Pokémon means "pocket monsters." There are LOTS of different pocket monsters, with names like Pikachu, Squirtle, and Jigglypuff.

2009: The Zhu Zhu Pets were a group of five little robot hamsters named Chunk, PipSqueak, Mr. Squiggles, Num Nums, and Patches. (Zhu Zhu means "little pig" in Chinese.) Besides being cute, they were also random. You couldn't predict which way the little fellows were going to scoot.

2011: Squinkies were squishy rubber toys that come in small plastic bubbles. The best part of these may have been the name. Try saying it in a really high voice: "Squinkies!" There were hundreds of Squinkie characters. They became so popular, stores had to limit how many a customer could buy.

Cute Quality: Paws and Limbs

Have you ever noticed that cute toys and stuffed animals have short arms and legs? Real arms usually hang at a person's sides, but a stuffed animal's arms are SO short, they often just pop straight out from its body.

The Usual! The Unusual!

Lots of the time, the stuffed animal doesn't really have a paw or a hand. Instead, its arm just sort of ends. I can't remember the last stuffed animal I saw with long arms and big hands and feet.

Of course, babies have short limbs with tiny hands and feet. But there's more than one path to cuteness. Have you ever seen a puppy with giant paws that seem too big for its body? Adorable!

We do want our cute animals to have the same number of limbs that we do: *Four!* This seems to leave spiders and snakes out of the cuteness sweepstakes. To check this, I was just looking at the ZooBorns.com website. It shows photos and information about ALL sorts of super-cute baby animals. Are there any animals they WON'T show? "We don't do a lot of insect larvae or spiders," says website creator Andrew Bleiman. You can guess why.

Cuteness Sells

As the Squinkies have taught us, cuteness sells! Of course, a cute toy sort of sells itself. But are the forces of cuteness powerful enough to sell UN-cute products?

Yes! Cuteness is used in ads for everything from car insurance to toilet paper. I mean, car insurance has to be one of the most boring things ever. To make their service interesting, the GEICO insurance company "went cute" by using a gecko in its ads back in 2000.

At first the GEICO gecko looked like a lizard and crawled on all four legs. Not bad, but could it be cuter? You bet! Slowly, the gecko was given bigger eyes, a rounder head, and a less-lizard-like look. Plus, it started standing upright and speaking with an accent. And that new, improved cute gecko has worked like a charm!

While car insurance isn't cute, cars can be. Take the VW Beetle. People loved the old classic Beetle because it was small and round and cute. Even its nickname was cute: the Bug!

When the Beetle was updated in 1998, VW made the car even *rounder*. They added a little flower vase on the dashboard. Cute! For a small car, the new Beetle sure has BIG head-lights. That's because it's designed so that the front of the car sort of looks like a smiling human face. (You know, the headlights are the eyes?) This gives it a friendly "face" in the front.

Other cars, like the Smart car, the Nissan Leaf, and the Mini Cooper, also have similar cute designs. They're all small and fun looking. The people who drive these cars aren't worried about being cool or tough. They'd rather be adorable!

Since I mentioned toilet paper earlier, the next time you're in the supermarket, find the toilet paper aisle. Notice anything? Almost all of the TP packages have little cherubs, friendly bears, and fluffy clouds. Why are toilet paper makers using cuteness? Probably to keep our mind off of the un-cute uses for TP!

Using cuteness in ads and packaging isn't always bad. For instance, if you look at bandages for kids, they come in colors like pink and tangerine. Some

Cute Quality: Roundness

Round things are cute! Don't believe me? Just pick the cuter of the paired items below!

Why rounded things are cute: If a puppy is roly-poly, the odds are that it's fat. The little guy needs all that fat to grow. Think about how fat human babies can be.

Also, straight lines and sharp corners are threatening. So are fangs and claws. So anything round is usually also harmless.

❖ **Ah-ha!** I never understood why people said "cute as a button" until now.

have little kittens or superheroes on them. The cute bandages cover the pain and help children forget it.

But there is a kind of "cute" ad I don't like: "saccharine ads." These are commercials that are full of fake sweetness. For example, any commercial that uses special effects to make a baby talk. Please! These people don't want us to think too hard about the cute tricks they're playing on us. I realized this when an advertiser said:

"Any ad featuring a baby—a delightfully cherubic and giggling baby at that—is {a sure thing}. You really can't lose—especially if he does an accent."

Ads like this can make ALL cute things seem shallow and cheap.

Advertisers will never stop mixing and matching cute qualities to try to sell us stuff. So it's up to us to understand the difference about the REAL and the FAKE cuteness around us. That way, we won't get tricked—and we won't let those meanies ruin cuteness either.

Boys and Cuteness

The odds are high that you are female. Why? Because girls are happy to learn about cute things. Boys, however, have to think about their image.

Boy 1: Look! Andre is reading a book about CUTE stuff.

Boy 2: Heheheh. He probably likes kittens.

Boy 1: Yeah.

Boy 2 (whispering): Actually, I sort of like kittens myself.

Boy 1 (relieved): Me too!

So while boys like cute stuff, they aren't as likely to show it. And the boys who are MOST worried about their image are the most likely to be anti-cute. They might say things like:

"Cuteness is marketing. It's just used to sell stuff."

For some types of cuteness, this is a good argument. But what is a puppy at the animal shelter selling besides happiness and love?

"Cuteness is lame. Let's listen to punk rock. And then hip-hop."

Punk rock is based on the idea of challenging other people's beliefs. So there is NOTHING MORE punk rock than a boy wearing pink. And you know who the original hip-hop artist is, right?

* **Interesting Thought** Many cute things, like babies and kittens, are practically begging to be taken care of. And women are most likely to provide that caring. So although men aren't immune from cuteness, maybe it makes sense that women do more "Oohing!" and "Aww-ing!"

Four Types of Cuteness

Since we're defining and thinking about cute stuff,
here are four specific *types* of cuteness that deserve
their own mention.

✳ 1. Ironic Cute ✳
Invented by "cool" people, funny people, hipsters

Let's face it: it's possible to overdose on cuteness.
Then all the rainbows and flowers in the world can
seem old and stale. Yes, puppies and kittens will
always be cute, but isn't there more to life than that?

Well, no.

Anyway, to keep cuteness fresh, some people
experiment with different kinds of cuteness. Like
ironic cute. You see, *irony* is the word we use for
things that are VERY different from what we expect,
so they are funny.

For example, imagine a sweet little koala
holding out its arms wide and saying, "*I hate you*

THIS much!" See, we don't expect the cute koala to say he HATES us, so it's funny.

Anything can be "ironic cute" if it's adorable, even as it gives us a little wink.

This is the kind of ironic cuteness that makes us smile—and then we say, "Seriously, give me the car keys!"

✳ 2. Nostalgia Cute ✳
Invented by people old enough to attend high school reunions

Some grumpy adults act like they don't care about cuteness. But, of course, they DO. And you can prove it.

If you know an adult's age, you can discover what was cute when that adult was a child. Let's say you have an uncle who grew up in the 1970s. Guess what? The comic strip called *Peanuts* was very popular then. And Snoopy (the dog) was probably the cutest Peanuts character.

So get a picture of Snoopy and ask your uncle to look at it.

"Aw, Snoopy!" he might chuckle. "Good old Snoopy. He sleeps on his dog house, you know."

See what happened? Your uncle remembers Snoopy is cute because:

Snoopy IS cute.

Snoopy reminds your uncle of his childhood.
What a happy time that was!

Things that remind us of our earlier lives give us a feeling called "nostalgia." And cute things often give us a feeling of happy nostalgia.

* **Quaintly Cute** Cute things SO old that nobody alive remembers them are called "quaint." Since these cute things aren't around anymore, we can only smile at their memory. (Example: the white dresses that little boys wore back in the 1800s are quaint.)

✳ 3. Sad Cuteness ✳
Invented by people who cry at movies and/or collect figurines

Do you like to have a good cry? Me neither! Even so, I've cried my eyes out watching *Dumbo*. You know the part where Dumbo's mom is locked in a cage? And she and Dumbo can only touch with their trunks?

sniff

Films with a lot of Sad Cuteness are called **tear-jerkers.** Like *Up!* It's about an old man who has trouble getting around, and an accident-prone boy who needs a father. These two meet an injured snipe bird. And if anything happens to that bird, then all

of its helpless babies will be
orphans!

✳ **Orphaned? Cute** We feel
   especially bad for orphans,
   so characters like Bambi get
   an Orphan Cuteness Bonus
   Score.

Helpless characters make
us feel sorry for them (p. 15). I
mean, look at the sad way that
little puppy is gazing at you!
How can you deny him a bite of your hot dog?

It's easy to overdo it with Sad Cuteness. For
example, have you ever seen "cute" little figurines of
children, angels, and animals? These small statues
gaze upward with big sad eyes and practically say,
"I'm so *small* and *pitiful*. Aren't I cute?"

No!

✳ 4. Bittersweet Cute ✳
Invented by weepy men

A bittersweet feeling is a pleasant sensation mixed
with sadness and pain. For example, my family used
to raise guide dogs for the blind. It was a lot of fun to
get puppies and then train them to follow commands.

But when the puppies became dogs, they had to leave our family and go elsewhere for more training. So getting a guide dog puppy was always bittersweet.

In *Toy Story 3*, the kid named Andy has grown up. Now he's ready to go to college. That means that Andy will be leaving his beloved toys behind.

Of course, we feel sorry for Andy's abandoned toys, which is why the man sitting next to me in the movie theater for *Toy Story 3* was crying like a baby. The poor toys were left all alone. I tried to tell the man it was only a cartoon, but he kept crying.

So I reminded the weeping man about *The House at Pooh Corner*. In this story, an older Christopher Robin says goodbye to Pooh and his childhood friends.

"But wherever they go, and whatever happens to them on the way, in that enchanted place on the top of the Forest, a little boy and his bear will always be playing."

"How bittersweet," the man said, wiping tears from his beard.

"*Exactly!*" I cried, high-fiving him.

Senior Cute

We know that babies are cute, but do we lose ALL of our cuteness as we get older?

No way! While it is harder to be cute as we age, it's not impossible. Look at Kin and Jin. These identical twin sisters were famous in Japan in the 1990s. They were 100 years old! Kin and Jin were constant guests on talk shows, and their faces were used to market lots of products.

Why were the twins such a big deal? Kin and Jin's talents were simply being small, defenseless, and adorable. They had high voices and said funny, old-fashioned things. Yep, the twins were *really cute*, and it didn't matter HOW old they were. They were two cute little old ladies.

Uh-oh. I guess the phrase

Who are you calling "cute little old ladies"?

"cute little old lady" is a bit disrespectful. A better word might be "sweet." But what's the difference between *cute* and *sweet*? Good question! Maybe "sweet" is for the things that warm our hearts that AREN'T exactly cute. For instance, when you see a car go by with a "Just Married" sign, it's not cute. It's a car. But it IS sweet, because it warms your heart.

Let's see if we can tell the difference between cute and sweet in the following examples:

A. An old man opening the door for some teenagers

B. A small-town parade on July 4th

C. A senior citizen swinging on a playground swing at the playground

D. An old woman holding a smiling baby

E. An older couple walking along and holding hands

F. A smiling old man

Sadly, it's harder for older men to qualify as cute, but don't despair! I've figured out a formula that may help them:

OLDER MEN + SMALL-SIZE CUTENESS + FURRINESS = GNOMES!

Answers: A. Sweet. B. Sweet. C. Cute, because of the contrast (p. 25) between the person's age and the activity! D. Cute. There's a baby, after all. But it can be sweet, too. E. Sweet. (Who doesn't get a good feeling from seeing older couples holding hands?) F. Uh-oh . . . neither?

Classic Cuteness

How Babies with Wings Get Around

Air Travel | Land Travel

Throughout history, mighty forces of cuteness have influenced why we say, "Awww!" I mean, haven't you ever wondered what the ancient people of our planet found cute back in the distant, misty past?

Babies, of course!

Also, people thought that flying things—like butterflies and birds—were cute. So at some point, a smart ancient person wondered, "What if an adorable baby had wings like a bird?"

A flying baby? That's genius! Of course, it's a little weird to think about a baby that can fly but not walk.

In modern times, we've all seen pictures or cartoons of flying babies. But did you know there are different kinds?

Cupid was the ancient Roman god of love and affection. He was usually shown as a boy with wings, holding a bow and some arrows. As you know, if someone was even scratched by one of Cupid's arrows, he or she would fall in love with whoever was close by.

Cherubs (or *cherubim*) are angels. But these angels were not originally babies. Instead, they looked like "adult" angel-people. During the Renaissance,[1] painters started showing winged babies in their artwork. And if the flying babies had halos over their heads, they were called "cherubs." If they didn't, they were called...

Putti (Latin for "little boys"), who are naked winged babies without halos. (Just one of the babies is a *putto*, but two or more give you *putti!*) Painting *putti* was a lot of fun. So when Valentine's Day came around, *putti* were rolled into the story of Cupid. And there have been Cupids flying all over the place ever since.

1. During this time, from the 1300s to 1600s, Europeans took a great interest in art and design.

Do you ♥ hearts?

People have thought of the heart as the home of emotions, like love, for a long time. But a ♥ doesn't look very much like a REAL heart, which is probably just as well.

Then why do we use the ♥ shape? Nobody knows for sure. One idea about this was inspired by the seeds of a plant called the silphium. Over 2,000 years ago, the silphium was linked with people who were in love. That's because the silphium's seeds really DO look like ♥s.

About 400 years ago, it became popular to use ♥s on Valentines. At first, the hearts were just on cards, but pretty soon they were everywhere.

♣ **Just Wondering** When you feel love for a puppy or a baby, that feeling is really in your brain. So shouldn't we draw little brains to show affection?

No matter what name you use for an airborne baby, that little newborn is almost always naked. This is based on the fact that REAL babies hate clothes. So in a lot of households, as a baby gets older and

becomes a toddler, it still seems natural to let the
baby run around naked.

* **Nudity Plus It helps make childhood free and
  innocent.**
* **Nudity Minus Kids without clothes will pee or poop
  anywhere, anytime.**

Of course, there IS an age limit for public nudity.
We've all been uncomfortably "exposed" to older kids
who still think it's fine to run around without clothes.

You: I see you're in your birthday suit.

Kid: Yep! Whoohoo!

You: How many birthdays has your suit had?

Kid: Seven! Whoohoo!

✳ The Superstar of Cuteness: Shirley Temple ✳

In the first part of the 1900s, television hadn't been invented. Of course, neither had the Internet. So cuteness fads moved pretty slowly. But as movies gained popularity, that started to change. And during the 1930s, a super-movie star of cuteness was born.

Although you may not have heard of her, Shirley Temple was the biggest child movie star EVER. What made Shirley special was that she was a cuteness quadruple-threat: she could act, sing, and dance AND she had dimples.

Shirley was only three years old when she appeared in her first film. Once people saw her, they LOVED her. Another thing that played up her cuteness was that Shirley almost always played cute, bouncy orphans who overcame hardship. Even the names of her characters were cute in a 1930s way, like "Lulu Parsnips" and "Dimples Appleby."

Shirley's career as a child star ended when she was 12. Of course, that makes sense, because you can't be a child star forever. As an adult, she became a U.S. ambassador. And I'm pretty sure that she was the only U.S. ambassador who could act, sing, and dance— AND had dimples.

Cute Classic: Pixies

Elves, fairies, and sprites are all great, but pixies are especially cute. Just look at their name: pixies. Based on that alone, they get major cuteness points.

Pixies have been around for thousands of years. It was believed that these small, magical beings were usually harmless to humans. Pixies were even known to be unexpectedly helpful to people who needed it. Since pixies loved kids, that meant getting help with chores.

♣ **Little-Known Fact:** Pixies are actually very neat and organized. That's why there is no such thing as "pixie lint." And "pixie dust" is only imaginary.

Seeing a pixie is thought of as good luck. If you're on the lookout, pixies have been described as ranging in size from a firefly to the size of an adult human. So, that narrows it down!

♣ **Littler-Known Fact:** Tinker Bell is NOT a pixie. In the original version of Peter Pan from 1904, she is a fairy.

✳ The Fairy Wedding ✳

Throughout history, "little people"[2] have often been treated as cute curiosities. So European kings and queens often included little people in their courts for entertainment. For example, a Polish ruler named Sigismund-Augustus had nine wee folk in his inner circle.

2. They were once known as midgets or pygmies.

This fascination helps explain an 1863 event called the Fairy Wedding. It was billed as the cutest event of the year: General Tom Thumb would marry his bride, Lavinia Bump.

Yes, it was the union of Thumb and Bump![3]

Tom and Lavinia were little people. Lavinia Bump was 32 inches tall, and Tom wasn't much bigger. With their dimples and high voices, the two of them were thought of as SO cute, people who saw them sometimes pinched themselves.

After all, Tom and Lavinia looked like children pretending to be adults. We know how cute that can seem (p. 23). Even so, the idea that little people are just naturally cute is insensitive in the same way as "cute little old ladies" (p. 135).

＊ **Cuteness Is in the Eye of the Pet Owner** Actress Sigourney Weaver arranged for her greyhound to marry a neighborhood dog. The ceremony included the line, *"Bark now or forever hold your peace."*

The newlywed couple were both entertainers. Tom and Lavinia's act included singing duets, dancing, and basically blowing people's minds with their cuteness. Their Fairy Wedding was the brainchild of P. T. Barnum.

As the owner of a famous big circus, Barnum was

3. The best man was George Washington Nutt. The bridesmaid was Lavinia's sister, Minnie Bump.

a businessman. And he made sure the Fairy Wedding earned a profit. After all, 2,000 people attended, and they were almost all charged admission.

Other businesspeople noticed the success of the Fairy Wedding. Cuteness could make money. This approach led to "commercial cuteness." That meant

Cute Things: Little Princesses

Back in the old days, princesses were few and far-between. That's because in any particular kingdom, you might only find ONE princess.

Things sure have changed. Today, we have almost NO kingdoms. Yet there are oodles of little girls who go through the "little princess" phase![4] Of course, kids have always *loved* to play make-believe. And as for being a princess, what's not to love?

PRINCESS PERKS
* Wearing beautiful clothes
* Princes are super-polite
* Going to fancy parties
* Being an authority figure (in pink)
* Free dance lessons

4. There are different types. The little girl might want to be a fairy or a princess ... or a fairy princess!

there would be some cute products (kitty calendars!)
and some UNcute ones. (Hello, Bratz dolls!)

* **Where'd You Get Those Peepers?** Imagine a life-
  sized Bratz doll. It would be scary! No creature on
  earth has eyes that big. I mean, Bratz eyes look like
  they take up 25% of the doll's face.

* Feeling like a queen (or a young one, anyway)
* Having a credit card for the Royal Treasury

In the modern day, Disney boosted the princess trend with
its VERY popular "Princess" line. This features famous characters from Disney cartoons, like Snow White, Pocahontas,
Ariel, Tiana, Princess Jasmine, Belle, Mulan, and Rapunzel.
Of course, not all of these young women are actual princesses, but never mind that!

* **What Is She Again?** Tinker Bell was originally part
  of the Princess line. But she was moved to the Disney
  "Fairies." (The difference is that the fairies are smaller
  than the princesses, and they have more "sass.")

It's worth knowing that there are over 25,000 different
Princess products made by Disney alone. Wow! Does that
leave room for a girl NOT to go through a princess phase?
It's an interesting question.

But I guess the important thing to remember is that when
it comes to phases, kids grow out of them.

Cute Classic

HIPPIES!

In the 1960s, many young people in the U.S. went through a unique phase. They called themselves hippies (or flower children), and they wanted to change the world to a simpler place. In this way, the hippies were similar to Japan's teenagers (p. 107).

From a fashion standpoint, hippies influenced what we think of as "cute" today.

* **Clothing:** Hippies wore bright, dyed fabrics—like tie-dye! Another hippie favorite was the bloopy, cartoony pattern called paisley. These patterns were cute AND weird.

* **Fuzzy-Furriness:** Hippies had hair. Lots and LOTS of hair. And flowers were sometimes stuck in those gigantic afros, manes, and mops.

* **Attitude:** Hippies liked words like "peace," "love," and "patchouli." One of their favorite sayings was "Flower Power." This shows that the hippies had positive attitudes and were generally harmless. (They did, however, smell like patchouli.)

Cutest Clothing: Footies

Anything that is *cuddly* can be cute. A baby tucked into its blanky? Yes. A kitten cuddled into a little ball on the sofa? Please! A dog that snuck under the warm laundry you just pulled out of the dryer?

Wow—that's REALLY cute.

But why should they have all the fun? We can get cuddly too. We just need some soft stuff to snuggle with . . . let's see, scarves, warm slippers—wait! I know. Nothing beats **pajamas**.

✷ **Persian PJs! The word "pajamas" from the Persian language. It combines "pa" (foot or leg) with "jama" (clothing), giving us *pajamas*: leg and foot clothing.**

Not only are pajamas soft and snuggly, but also their nickname is cute: PJs! And of all the pajamas available, the cutest ones are *onesies*. These are the little one-piece outfits that babies wear that cover their whole bodies . . . AND their feet.

Toddlers can also wear onesies, although then we often called them something like "footed sleepers."

It turns out that there are LOTS of names for these pajamas!

* footies, footsie or feetsie PJs
* nightie
* one-piece pajamas
* zip-up jammies
* sleeper suit
* sherpa sleeper
* walking blanket
* walking blanket
* walking sleeper
* sleeper walker

But it doesn't really matter what name you use. If you've ever seen a kid in footies run down a hardwood hallway and then slide while giggling crazily, you know how awesome these PJs are!

The award for the cutest kind of onesie, however, is the **bunny suit**. These are pink or white pajamas with a puffball tail and a hood with bunny ears. They combine the cuteness of a bunny with the beauty of a onesie.

Cuteness Ratings

As we know, cuteness can be defined with "Cuteness Qualities." On the next page is a chart that includes most of them.

Just use a 1–5 scoring system (with 5 as the high score), for rating. Then average the scores together to get an overall "cuteness rating."

Is this the final word on cuteness? Nope! There was only room for limited contestants, so I had to leave out hamsters. And ladybugs.

Also, I weighted the Cuteness Qualities equally. But you might think some categories are more important than others.

And different people will score differently. Speaking of people, you can always use this chart to rate your brother, sister, or best friend. (I'm sure he or she will thank you. ☺)

CONTESTANT	Young	Small	Waddles	Chubby-Rounded	Fuzzy-Furry	Cuddle Factor	Big Head
Baby otter	3	3	4	4	5	2	
Duckling							
Puppy							
Koala			—				
Panda bear cub							
Baby (8 months old)							
Baby penguin							
Baby bunny			♣				
Baby hedgehog							
Harbor seal pup			—				
Baby monkey							
Cherub			—				
Kitten							
Baby goat							
Baby elephant						—	

Before I filled in this chart, I was sure the Cuteness Champion would be the human baby. I thought second place would go to the duckling or the otter. Go figure! According to my numbers, the top three cutest things are babies, puppies, and . . . *drum roll* BABY BUNNIES!

Cute Eyes	Cute Ears	Cute Nose, Mouth	Cute Limbs	Harmless	Helpless	Makes Cute Sounds	Cute Colors	Cute Attitude	Cuteness Score
4	4	5	5	2	5	4	4	6	3.93
	—								
						*			
	—								
						—			
			♥						
			✳						

* FYI, koalas snore, belch, and bellow. Pandas bleat, honk, and squeal. And hedgehogs snuffle, whistle, snort, purr, chirp, and squeak!

♣ Bunnies hop. That is totally cute!

♥ Armed and dangerous! (You know, the bow and arrows?)

* Long, knobby legs are cute! (See colts, baby giraffes, baby antelope, etc.)

Cuteness Review and
Final Test

So is cuteness just eye candy? It can be. But remember, the best cuteness can be heart and brain candy too.

I really like the types of cuteness that give us a good feeling AND make us think. For instance, walking our dog at the park, I went past the play area and stopped to watch the kids having fun.

I noticed one little girl who would stop playing every so often. She would turn her

head away from her friends, and then smile. Then she would go back to playing.

"Hi," I said. "Do you mind if I ask why you're smiling over there?"

The girl looked over and said, "Oh, I'm smiling at the trees."

Cuteness Alert! A little kid smiling at trees is impossibly adorable. And what was going through her mind when she did this? That's a bonus: The girl gave me something to think about, too.

And since we're thinking, you're finally ready to learn the different Cuteness Levels. Hurray!

Cuteness Level 1: *Cute!*
Example: A sleeping child.
Your example: _____

Cuteness Level 2: *The Cuteness vortex begins to pull you in!*
Example: A puppy playing with a teddy bear.
Your example: _____

Cuteness Level Three: *Multiplying Cuteness*
Example: A four-year old boy in pajamas coochie-coos a smiling baby.
Your example: _____

Cuteness Level Four: *You can't HANDLE the Cuteness!*
Example: A puppy and a kitten wrestle while a baby in a onesie watches from behind a teddy bear.
Your example: _____

Cuteness Level Five: *The Cuteness! It burns!*
Example: A toddler pushes a stroller full of sleeping kittens and puppies to a birthday party for a bunny. Behind the stroller, a line of ducklings follow.[1]
Your example: _____

---

1. This has never actually happened. If it did, the world, as we know it, would
cease to exist.

✳ Cute Final ✳

This exam is designed to test your knowledge of all things cute. If you do not pass this test, you will NOT be considered an authority on cuteness.

This will be a crushing blow to your self-esteem, which would not be very cute at all!

Time Allotted: 30 minutes

STOP! Do not turn this page unless you are prepared to take the test. Once you begin, there is no turning back . . . and no re-takes are allowed!

Now, take a deep breath. Think of a baby pushing some kittens in stroller. And you better throw in some bunny rabbits just to be safe.

Okay?

Begin!

Yay! You passed!

Sorry to freak you out with all that "exam" stuff. But don't you feel a greater sense of accomplishment when you finish a book this way?

Look, the world can be tough. So go forth and make it a cuter—and happier—place!

Bibliography

Amini, Fari, Thomas Lewis, and Richard Lannon. *A General Theory of Love*. New York: Vintage, 2001.

Angier, Natalie. "The Cute Factor." *The New York Times*, January 3, 2006.

"A Masterpiece of Nature? Yuck!" *The New York Times*, August 9, 2010.

Anthes, Emily. "Youngsters Immune to the Contagious Yawn." *Scientific American*, January 11, 2011.

Antonakis, John and Olaf Dalgas. "Predicting Elections: Child's Play!" *Science*, February 27, 2009.

Avella, Natalie. *Graphic Japan*. East Sussex, UK: Rotovision, 2004.

"Baby flamingos 'scared of pink'." *The Telegraph*, June 18, 2009.

Bloom, Paul. "The Moral Lives of Babies." *The New York Times Magazine*, May 5, 2010.

"British doctors warn against 'designer dimple' cosmetic surgery." News.com.au, June 22, 2010.

Buchen, Lucy. "Meerkats Don't Spoil Their Mind-Numbingly Cute Babies." Wired.com, May 22, 2009.

Demetriou, Danielle. "Hello Kitty-themed maternity hospital opens in Taiwan." *The Telegraph*, December 8, 2008.

Deroy, Ophelia. "Why Pink?" The International Culture and Cognition Institute (www.cognitionandculture.net), September 6, 2010.

Eibl-Eibesfeldt, Irenäus. *Ethology: The Biology of Behavior*. New York: Holt, Rineholt and Winston, 1970.

Fine, Cordelia. *Delusions of Gender: How Our Minds, Society, and Neurosexism Create Difference*. New York: W.W. Norton & Company, 2010.

Garger, Ilya. "One Nation, Under Cute." *Psychology Today*, March 1, 2007.

Genosko, Gary. "Natures and Cultures of Cuteness." *Invisible Culture: An Electronic Journal for Visual Studies*, Fall 2005.

Gould, Stephen Jay. *The Panda's Thumb: More Reflections on Natural History*. New York: Norton, 1980.

Grossman, Lev. "Creating a Cute Cat Frenzy." *Time*, July 12, 2007.

Haber, Matt. "Killing Me Softly." Observer.com, June 10, 2008.

Harris, Daniel. *Cute, Quaint, Hungry and Romantic: The Aesthetics of Consumerism*. New York: Da Capo Press, 2000.

Herzog, Hal. *Some We Love, Some We Hate, Some We Eat: Why It's So Hard to Think Straight About Animals*. New York: Harper, 2010.

Jackson, Kate M. "Why is this pink hat so hated?" *The Boston Globe*, June 26, 2008.

"Japanese culture is becoming a cult of cute." Associated Press, June 14, 2006.

Keim, Brandon. "Babies Want to Be Social, Even Before They're Born." Wired.com, October 8, 2010.

Kitten War. http://kittenwar.com

Klass, Perri. "Understanding 'Ba Ba Ba' as a Key to Development." The New York Times, October 11, 2010.

Koh, Barbara, et al. "Cute Power!" *Newsweek* (Pacific Edition), November 8, 1999.

Ksepka, Daniel. "5 things you never knew about penguins!" *Scientific American*, December 20, 2010.

Laurent, Erik L. "Mushi." *Natural History*, March 2001.

Lipman, Gregg. "The Cute Route." *Brandweek*, January 12, 2009.

Lorenz, Konrad, and P. Leuhausen. *Motivation of Human and Animal Behavior*. New York: Van Nostrand Reinhold, 1973.

—. The *Foundations of Ethology*. New York: Springer-Verlag, 1981.

Mangum, Aja. "Glitter: A Brief History." *New York Magazine*, October 7, 2007.

Manning, Sue. "Awww...animal babies make conservation cute." The Associated Press, October 29, 2010.

McDonell, Keelin. "The Shape of My Heart." Slate.com, February 13, 2007.

McDowell, Margaret A., and company. "Anthropometric Reference Data for Children and Adults: United States, 2003–2006." *National Health Statistics Reports*. Hyattsville, MD: National Center for Health Statistics, October 22, 2008.

"Mind: The Science, Art, and Experience of Our Inner Lives." The Exploratorium, Palace of Fine Arts, San Francisco, 2010 (www.exploratorium.edu/mind/judgment)

Ngai, Sianne. "The Cuteness of the Avant-Garde." *Critical Inquiry*, Volume 31, No. 4.

Orenstein, Peggy. "What's Wrong With Cinderella?" *The New York Times*, December 24, 2006.

Pastoureau, Michel. *The Devil's Cloth: A History of Stripes*. Washington: Washington University Press, 2003.

Paul, Annie Murphy. "Is Pink Necessary?" *The New York Times*, January 21, 2011.

Paumgarten, Nick. "Master of Play." *The New Yorker*, December 20, 2010.

Peterson, Nicole. Design Benign: www.design-benign.com

Poliquin, Rachel. "The Visual Erotics of Mini-Marriages." *The Believer*, November/December 2007.

Prieto, Bianca. "Suspicious 'FurReal' pony blown up near elementary school." *Orlando Sentinel*, September 7, 2010.

Roach, Mary. "Cute Inc." Wired.com, December 1999.

Rohrer, Finlo. "A new type of tear-jerker." BBC News, July 16, 2010.

Richard, Frances. "Fifteen Theses on the Cute." *Cabinet Magazine*, Fall 2001.

Sanders, John T. "On 'Cuteness.'" *The British Journal of Aesthetics*, April 1992.

Sherman, Gary D., Jonathan Haidt, and James A. Coan. "Viewing cute images increases behavioral carefulness." *Emotion*, April 2009.

Sohn, Emily. "Color Preferences Determined by Experience." Discovery News (www.news.discovery.com), October 1, 2010.

Stewart, Jude. "Seeing Spots. From lepers to paranoia: The twisted history of the polka dot." Slate.com, September 10, 2010.

Thomson, Rosemarie Garland. *Freakery: Cultural Spectacles of the Extraordinary Body*. New York: New York University Press, 1996.

Vince, Gaia. "Guinea pig power." WanderingGaia.com, September 5, 2010.

Williamson, Eugenia. "The story of pink." *The Boston Globe*, July 11, 2010.

Windolf, Jim. "Addicted to Cute." *Vanity Fair*, December 2009.